Federal Evaluation Policy

Analyzing the Effects of Public Programs

by
Joseph S. Wholey
John W. Scanlon
Hugh G. Duffy
James S. Fukumoto
Leona M. Vogt

The Urban Institute
Washington, D.C.

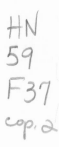
SBN No. 87766-003-4
Library of Congress Catalog Card No. 78-139578
UI 9-121-21   1970   2nd printing, 1971

Available from:

Publications Office
The Urban Institute
2100 M Street, N.W.
Washington, D. C. 20037

List price: $2.95

Printed in the United States of America

Foreword

How well do federal programs for treating urban problems succeed in their aim? This question constantly recurs to city officials, Congress, and specialists in urban affairs. It is raised most keenly, perhaps, by just those federal agencies that conduct the programs.

To learn the answer to that question, one needs a system for measuring what is working and what is not. Without the ability to gauge performance, criticisms are uninformed, solutions largely guesswork. The men who are charged with making and executing policy know this. At the same time, many of them have the uncomfortable feeling that the art of evaluating programs and managerial practices is a neglected one.

Two years ago The Urban Institute, supported by funds from the Department of Housing and Urban Development, decided to begin an evaluation of the federal government's ability to evaluate. This study is the result.

It confirms what many had suspected. The art and techniques of evaluation are indeed underdeveloped. For that reason the study tries to go beyond describing the problem: it also gives a good deal of attention to the way present evaluation methods might be improved. The findings and recommendations were made available to the agencies studied and to the Executive Office of the President. Considerable follow-up activity has resulted, often with the assistance of Institute staff.

Events have overtaken a number of the details reported here. In most public agencies, however, little change in evaluation practices has occurred in the past year. It is our hope in publishing this study that the general approach to program evaluation described here will be useful to administrators and legislative bodies, to the state and local officials who carry out federal programs, and to the analysts both in and outside government who will be perfecting evaluation tools in the years to come.

WILLIAM GORHAM
President
The Urban Institute

Washington, D. C.
June, 1970

Table of Contents

Foreword 5

Preface 11

Acknowledgments... 13

1. Introduction... 15
   Scope of This Study.. 17

2. Federal Evaluation—What It Is and Why It Is Needed........... 19
   Many Programs, Uncertain Results.................................... 20
   Major Kinds of Evaluation.. 23
       Evaluation Defined... 23
       Program-Project Distinction 24
       Types of Evaluation 24
           Program Impact Evaluation.............................. 25
           Program Strategy Evaluation............................ 25
           Project Evaluation.. 25
           Project Rating.. 25
       Evaluation Alternatives 26
           Field Experiments... 26
           Experimental Demonstrations............................ 26
       Evaluation-Related Activities 27
           Monitoring 27
           Reporting Systems 27
           Cost Analysis.. 27

3. Administration of an Evaluation System 28
  Definition of Program Objectives 28
    Agency Role 30
    Role of Program Managers and Evaluators 31
    Positive and Negative Side Effects 33
    Data Reporting Requirements 34
    Recommendations 1-6 .... *35*
  Developing Work Plans 35
    Best Work Plans Found in OEO 36
    Other Agency Efforts 39
    Cost of Failure to Plan 40
    Recommendations 7-14 .... *40*
  Design and Execution of Studies 42
    Contract Hazards 42
    Requests for Proposals 44
    Contract Monitoring 44
    Recommendations 15-16 .... *45*
  Dissemination and Use of Evaluation Studies 46
    Studies Without Impact 46
    Some Influence Felt 48
    Major Roadblocks 50
    Recommendations 17-22 .... *51*

4. Organizational Relationships and Responsibilities 52
  Congress 53
    Recommendations 23-26 .... *57*
  The Executive Office 58
    Recommendations 27-31 .... *59*
  Federal Agencies 61
    The OEO Model 62
      High-Level Support 63
      Location of Agency-Level Evaluation 63
      Staff Concentration on Evaluation 65
      Coordinating Role 65
    Program-Level View 67
    Recommendations 32-39 .... *69*
  State and Local Levels 73
    Recommendations 40-43 .... *75*

5. Evaluation Resources 77
   Funds 77
      Recommendations 44-47 .... *81*
   Staffing 82
      Recommendations 48-54 .... *84*

6. Methodology 86
   Potential of Research Design and Method 87
   Sampling Equivalent "Experimental" and "Control"   89
   Groups 89
      Recommendations 55-58 .... *93*
   Defining Effectiveness Criteria and Measuring Effects 93
   Monitoring 95
   Follow-Up 96
      Recommendations 59-61 .... *97*
   Isolation and Control of Treatments 97
   Program Impact, Program Strategy and
      Local Project Evaluation 98
   Planned Variation 100
   Project Rating 101
   Evaluation-Related Activities 103
      Recommendations 62-71 .... *104*
   Feasibility of Evaluation 106
      Recommendation 72 .... *110*

7. Summary of Major Recommendations 111
   Role of the Executive Office 111
   Leadership 111
   Priorities 112
   Federal Evaluation System 112
   Requests for Resources 113
   Role of the Congress 113
   National Impact Evaluations 113
   Program Strategy Evaluation 113
   Role of the Federal Agencies 114
   Agency Head Support 114
   Evaluation Plan 114
   Types of Evaluation 115

Methodology 116
Organizational Responsibilities.................................116
Funding..117
Staff 117
Role of Program Offices 118
Administration of Evaluation 118
Types of Evaluation 119

Select Bibliography *121*

Tables

1. Paradigm for OEO Program Impact Evaluations.................. 37
2. Recommended Assignment of Major Evaluation
    Responsibilities for Selected Programs 71
3. 1969 Funding and In-House Staff for
    Evaluation of Selected Programs 79
4. Variations in Evaluation Research Designs 88
5. Methodological Feasibility of Evaluation 107
6. Preliminary Estimates of Existing Conditions for
    Evaluation of Selected Federal Programs............................109

Preface

Evaluation is becoming increasingly important in the development of federal social policies and in the management of federal social programs. To make certain that these policies and programs meet the needs of society, it is necessary to analyze programs to determine their consequences—that is, to measure their successes and failures in meeting the nation's goals. The federal government has only begun to develop the methodologies and systems that produce such assessments.

The Urban Institute undertook this study of federal evaluation policies, concentrating on the organizational framework, the methodologies and the amount of federal resources used at the time the review began in late 1968. This study, funded by the Department of Housing and Urban Development, was conducted in close cooperation with the Executive Office of the President and the four agencies examined—the Department of Housing and Urban Development, the Office of Economic Opportunity, the Department of Health, Education and Welfare, and the Department of Labor. The Urban Institute completed an overview of its findings and recommendations in September 1969, and circulated a draft of this paper to officials in the Executive Office and the agencies involved.

The following changes have taken place since September 1969, which reflect or parallel recommendations made in the study:

White House: The President on March 12, 1970, presented a reorganization plan, subsequently accepted by the Congress, which would enhance the capabilities of the Bureau of the Budget to conduct evaluation, especially across agency lines.

11

Office of Economic Opportunity: The Office of Legal Services has developed an on-site evaluation system to improve its project monitoring capabilities.

Department of Health, Education, and Welfare: The Office of the Assistant Secretary for Planning and Evaluation for the first time has been given the resources to conduct major evaluation studies and is now playing an important role in reviewing agency evaluation plans. The U. S. Office of Education is devoting considerable attention to evaluation in relation to Title I of the Elementary and Secondary Education Act.

Department of Labor: The Assistant Secretary for Policy, Evaluation and Research has begun to play an important role in planning departmental evaluation efforts. Staff of this office and of the Manpower Administration are planning evaluation of state manpower programs under the Administration's proposed decentralization plan.

Department of Housing and Urban Development: The Office of the Secretary of Housing and Urban Development is paying increased attention to planning and execution of departmental evaluation efforts.

The Urban Institute has been requested to take a continuing role in much of this new evaluation work. The Institute is working closely with OEO's Office of Legal Services, with a Title I Elementary and Secondary Education Task Force appointed by the Commissioner of Education, with the Office of Planning, Research and Evaluation in the Office of Education, with the Labor Department's Manpower Administration staff, and with the Model Cities Administration of the Department of Housing and Urban Development to assist in a number of evaluation projects.

A companion piece to this report, entitled "Evaluation within the Office of Economic Opportunity," consolidates much of the OEO experience with evaluation cited in this larger report. It is available as a working paper at The Urban Institute. Material gathered about evaluation practices in the other federal agencies studied is on file at the Institute.

Acknowledgments

This report was prepared by Joseph S. Wholey, project director, and John W. Scanlon, Hugh G. Duffy, James S. Fukumoto and Leona M. Vogt. Other Urban Institute staff members who contributed to the study were Martin A. Berlin, William C. Copeland, Ralph Smith and Jaroslawa C. Zelinsky. Two consultants, Michael Kirst and John Frantz, prepared papers on Office of Education and Department of Housing and Urban Development programs, respectively. Walter Rybeck was editor, with Warren T. Greenleaf and John Greenya assisting in an initial version of this report.

Valuable comments and suggestions were made by Jack Carlson, Frank Lewis, Richard Nathan and Paul O'Neill of the Bureau of the Budget; Keith Marvin of the General Accounting Office; John Cheston, Saul Hoch, William Kolberg and Alfred Zuck of the Department of Labor; James Abert, Jack Biren, Mary Jane Cronin, Ruth Hanft, Wayne Kimmel, Howard Matthews and Philip M. Timpane of the Department of Health, Education and Welfare; James Cowhig, Richard Langendorf and George Wright of the Department of Housing and Urban Development; John Evans and Gerald Sparer of the Office of Economic Opportunity; Curtis Aller, San Francisco State College; Ruth Covell, University of California Medical School; Henry Dyer, Educational Testing Service; Bernard Frieden, Massachusetts Institute of Technology; Donald Kummerfeld, Center for Political Research; Alice Rivlin, the Brookings Institution; Gordon Sutton, University of Massachusetts; Carol Weiss, Columbia University; Walter Williams, National

13

Manpower Policy Task Force; and Harvey Garn, Harry Hatry, Charles Holt, Morton Isler, Joseph Lewis, Selma Mushkin, Antoine Perot, Gilbert Ware and Bayla White of the Urban Institute.

Innumerable drafts of project working papers and the final manuscript were typed by Isabelle Duke, Mary Sarley, Claudia Sargeant, and Elaine Worsley.

1. Introduction

The most impressive finding about the evaluation of social programs in the federal government is that substantial work in this field has been almost nonexistent.

Few significant studies have been undertaken. Most of those carried out have been poorly conceived. Many small studies around the country have been carried out with such lack of uniformity of design and objective that the results rarely are comparable or responsive to the questions facing policy makers.

There is nothing akin to a comprehensive federal evaluation system. Even within agencies, orderly and integrated evaluation operations have not been established. Funding has been low. Staffing has been worse, forcing undue reliance on outside contractors by agencies that lack the in-house capacity to monitor contract work. The most clear-cut evidence of the primitive state of federal self-evaluation lies in the widespread failure of agencies even to spell out program objectives. Unless goals are precisely stated, there is no standard against which to measure whether the direction of a program or its rate of progress is satisfactory.

The impact of activities that cost the public millions, sometimes billions, of dollars has not been measured. One cannot point with confidence to the difference, if any, that most social programs cause in the lives of Americans. It has not been established that one approach has been more effective than another in reducing poverty, eliminating slums or providing quality education to all children. Why the same type of project seems to succeed in one community but fails in another has not been determined. Lack of a solid, scientific information base about past and present programs poses severe limitations on the federal government's ability to map out sound future programs.

Dismal as this record appears, there has been a start. The best example of an evaluation system was found in the Office of Economic Opportunity. Other agencies have undertaken or begun useful work in certain phases of evaluation. Congress in several instances has insisted that agencies justify their spending requests by first assessing the effectiveness of programs already under way. Some funds and staff have been allocated, and coordination efforts have begun.

Enough good, useful results have emerged on the plus side of the evaluation picture to indicate the potential value of a full-scale effort. By pulling together the best approaches that have been carried out or proposed throughout the many federal agencies and programs studied, it is possible to describe the basic elements that should be incorporated into a useful evaluation system.

Evaluation should examine policies and programs from the broadest national level down to specific operations of projects at the local level, including their impact on individuals. A range of types of evaluation is needed to focus on these different targets.

To accomplish the required evaluation tasks requires adequate funds and sufficient personnel with necessary technical background. Since it is not anticipated that the federal government can operate the entire evaluation system without considerable reliance on contract work, in-house staff must be assigned to design, monitor and coordinate outside efforts.

Each level of the federal government should develop an evaluation work plan covering at least the most important social programs. These plans should look ahead two or three years and should be revised periodically to be kept relevant to decision-making needs.

Not everything one might want to investigate in federal programs can be evaluated. There are questions that should not be pursued—study cost may be out of line, results might not be obtainable by the time answers are needed, or feasible methods may not exist for tracing certain kinds of effects. It is essential, therefore, to know the limits of what evaluation can accomplish. Improving methodologies also is a vital function of a comprehensive evaluation system.

Finally, evaluation findings should be widely disseminated and put to use. This will be a self-reinforcing process. When top policy leaders—whether in the White House, Bureau of the Budget, Congress, departments or program manager offices—are seen to give or withhold funds and to expand or alter program content as a result of evaluation, the art of systematic assessment is bound to be enhanced.

The emphasis is not on an evaluation system for its own sake, but on the development of a necessary, useful tool for improving social programs supported by the federal government.

SCOPE OF THIS STUDY

This report examines the present system for federal evaluation of social programs. It offers findings and recommendations on the administration, the resources, and the organizational arrangements needed to facilitate various types of evaluation of public social programs.

Herein are presented the results of the Urban Institute's examination of the status of evaluation in 15 programs conducted by four Federal agencies (the Department of Health, Education and Welfare, the Department of Housing and Urban Development, the Department of Labor, and the Office of Economic Opportunity), the Bureau of the Budget, and the General Accounting Office. The 15 sample programs are the following:

    HEW—Maternal and Child Health
            Vocational Education
            Title I of the Elementary and Secondary Education
                Follow Through Act
    HUD—Model Cities
            Urban Renewal
            Urban Planning Assistance
    DOL—Manpower Development and Training
            Neighborhood Youth Corps
            Job Opportunities in the Business Sector
            Work Incentive Program

OEO—Head Start[1]
         Job Corps[1]
         Community Action Program
         Legal Services Program

The sample represents a range of evaluation efforts. The average program in the sample probably reflects evaluation activity above the average for the federal government as a whole.

Information for the study was collected through discussions with policy makers, program managers and evaluators; and through examination of agency research and evaluation policies, procedures, plans and completed studies.

---

1. After completion of the data-collection phase of the study, Head Start was transferred to the Department of Health, Education and Welfare, and the Job Corps was transferred to the Department of Labor.

2. Federal Evaluation — What It Is and Why It Is Needed

Evaluation is a necessary foundation for effective implementation and judicious modification of our existing programs. At this point, evaluation is probably more important than the addition of new laws to an already extensive list of educational statutes. . . . Evaluation will provide the information we require to strengthen weak programs, fully support effective programs, and drop those which simply are not fulfilling the objectives intended by the Congress when the programs were originally enacted. — The Honorable Robert H. Finch (165)*

This study focuses on one of the tools used in the federal decision-making process: *formal, organized evaluation* of federal programs and projects. In this sense, evaluation is research, the application of the scientific method to experience with public programs to learn what happens as a result of program activities. Evaluation includes the definition of program objectives, the development of measures of progress toward these objectives, the assessment of what difference public programs actually make, and the projection of what reasonably could be expected if the programs were continued or expanded.

The essence of evaluation is the comparison of both outcome—what happened that would not have happened in the absence of the program?—and relative effectiveness—what strategies or projects within programs work best? The purpose of evaluation is to provide objective information to program managers and policy

*Numbers in parentheses refer to bibliographic sources beginning on page 121.

makers on the costs and effects of national programs and local projects, thereby assisting in effective management and efficient allocation of limited resources.

Social programs such as the Title I program for elementary and secondary education of disadvantaged children, manpower development and training programs, and the Model Cities program are designed on the assumption that certain courses of action will improve education, increase employment and income, or reverse the process of urban decay. However, relatively little is known about the effectiveness of such programs in meeting their objectives. Overcoming this lack of information is impeded by the severe problems in developing and executing evaluation studies. Among these problems are the difficulties of defining social program objectives and output measures, methodological, bureaucratic, and practical constraints, shortages of trained personnel, lack of funds, and the absence of clearly defined evaluation policies.

MANY PROGRAMS, UNCERTAIN RESULTS

Since the 1930s, the performance of the national economy has been the primary domestic concern of the federal government. Although the economy is still of paramount importance, the government has in the past decade given increased attention to national social goals and problems. The reasons are clear—along with our rapid economic growth have come urban decay, skill obsolescence, environmental pollution, growing social unrest, and the awareness of poverty amid affluence. The recent proliferation of federal programs concerned with human resource development and improvement in the quality of life has been in response to our multiplying social ills.

The past decade has made the nation aware of the need to set priorities among domestic problems and to plan their solutions carefully. To meet most of our major needs—in housing, education, manpower training, or other areas of national concern—will require massive commitments of money and manpower over long periods of time. The increased competition for limited resources makes it imperative to examine critically the social and economic benefits associated with what we are doing and what we plan to do.

In addition to this problem of scarce resources, there is a growing concern with the actual effects that domestic federal policies and expenditures have on individuals, groups, neighborhoods and communities. Traditionally, the federal government has been much more concerned with the efficiency of its programs than with their negative and positive effects. The public assistance programs, for example, are managed under a system that is "audit" and "compliance" oriented. Case workers see to it that eligibility requirements are met; and the operating agencies see to it that money goes where it is intended. For many years, little consideration was given to the impact of this system on either the "beneficiaries" or society. The consequences of any particular federal program subtly and indirectly affect much more of society than the intended recipients. Certainly, the larger society will continue to pay for the family disintegration that has been caused by dysfunctional public assistance programs. For most other social programs, it is not usually known who is or is not benefiting and to what degree. Consequently, the outcomes of federal programs are beginning to be questioned. Once it was enough to know that so many federal dollars bought so many miles of highway; now there is concern with "secondary" impacts, such as the effects on community residents and the ecology.

Experience with social planning teaches that two factors must be kept in mind when developing and carrying out federal programs: any course of action has many possible outcomes and any act has inherent error associated with it. We cannot predict with certainty which results will follow from particular policies, nor should we be confident that policy implementation will conform to plan. Both factors imply that early determination of effects is necessary in order to meet, and possibly redirect, program goals. The limited resources available to meet grave social needs and the significant but largely unpredictable impact of federal domestic policies require timely feedback about both positive and negative effects from on-going programs to assure productive program planning and management.[2]

---

2. "Feedback refers to the total information process through which primary and second-order effects of organizational actions are fed back to the organization and compared with desired performance." Robert A. Rosenthal and Robert S. Weiss (6).

The main concern here is in evaluation systems that make possible more objective judgments on the economic and social costs and effects of national programs and local projects. These judgments can be used by policy makers as guides to broad resource allocation and major policy decisions, and by managers to make better choices among projects, program strategies and techniques.

Evaluation of a sort has been going on in the federal government for a long time. Program managers and policy makers have always made judgments about the value of programs and of projects. However, the federal government as a whole and most federal agencies have no overall *system* for objectively evaluating program and project effectiveness.

For most federal social programs, objectives have not been established, output measures have not been selected, reporting systems have not yielded information on the effects of programs or even on progress toward short-term objectives. There is no system for planning, executing and using evaluation studies.

To date, few if any programs have been sufficiently well evaluated to allow confident estimates of the benefits that would follow from budget level changes or reallocations within programs. The Office of Economic Opportunity has undertaken a number of studies to throw light on national program effectiveness. The first of these studies to be completed strongly suggested that Head Start programs have been generally ineffective in improving disadvantaged children's long-term cognitive development (174). The Department of Health, Education and Welfare studies of the Title I Elementary and Secondary Education program suggest that the program is not generally effective in improving disadvantaged children's achievement. Both of these findings imply the need for the federal government—and the nation—to learn more about what types of preschool and school programs can succeed and under what sets of conditions they are most likely to do so. The current experimental demonstration programs for primary education of disadvantaged children (the Follow Through program) and for pre-school education of disadvantaged children (within Head Start) are direct responses to the evidence that certain Title I and Head Start programs were ineffective in important respects (153).

Evaluation, of course, is no panacea. Formal evaluation studies are and will continue to be only a part of the process of getting information relevant and necessary to decision making. Even if we had sound information on the effectiveness of existing programs and projects in achieving a variety of public objectives, there would still remain differences of opinion over how much effort to assign each of the objectives. Nevertheless, more enlightened decisions can be made by those who get good information on program effectiveness.

Progress has been made in recent years in improving the whole federal decision-making process. Congress has been increasingly concerned about evaluating existing federal programs. In recent years, certain major legislation has included both the requirement for evaluation and the funding for carrying it out. Also, the Executive branch has attempted since 1965 to improve program planning through analytical studies on key policy questions under the Planning-Programming-Budgeting (PPB) system. Yet, the whole federal machinery for making policy and budget decisions suffers from a crucial weakness: it lacks a comprehensive system for measuring program effectiveness. With uncertainty about the effects of past and present programs, it is difficult if not impossible to be efficient in planning or in allocating funds to future programs.

MAJOR KINDS OF EVALUATION

Evaluation Defined

Evaluation as discussed in this report has several distinguishing characteristics relating to focus, methodology and function. The following operational description clarifies these characteristics:

> Evaluation (1) assesses the *effectiveness* of an *on-going* program in achieving its objectives, (2) relies on the principles of research design to distinguish a program's effects from those of other forces working in a situation, and (3) aims at program improvement through a modification of current operations.

Note that evaluation is concerned with questions of program effectiveness more than program efficiency. In this respect, it is goal-oriented, focusing on output rather than input. Evaluation's preoccupation with existing programs differs from "program analysis" and "policy analysis" which usually compare existing *and* hypothetical alternative program solutions to the same problem. Evaluation's function is to provide feedback from results to decisions. It is the activity that links program operations to planning and programming. Evaluation findings can be used to modify current operations and to plan future programs and policies. It provides information for the incremental upgrading of a program, or groups of programs with similar objectives.

Program-Project Distinction

Federal agencies usually provide support to intermediaries, such as states, cities, school districts, local housing authorities and hospitals. These in turn provide services directly to ultimate beneficiaries. The organizations directly providing services, on the other hand, may receive support from a number of state or local sources as well as from the federal government. Both these facts complicate the task of evaluating federal programs. Consequently, certain distinctions must be made in discussions of federal evaluation efforts:

As used in this report, a federal *program* is defined as the provision of federal funds and administrative direction to accomplish a prescribed set of objectives through the conduct of specified activities. Typically the federal money goes to intermediaries rather than to final recipients of services.

A *project* is the implementation level of a program—the level where resources are used to produce an end product that directly contributes to the objectives of the program.

A distinction therefore is made throughout this report between, for example, the national Head Start *program* and local Head Start *projects*. In a very few federal programs, such as Medicare, the federal government itself also takes the role of a project agency and serves as its own intermediary. Such programs are rare, however.

Types of Evaluation

We distinguish four major types of evaluation—program impact evaluation, program strategy evaluation, project evaluation, and project rating.[3]

---

3. These definitions are based, in part, on OEO's distinction among types of program evaluations. See Chapter 4 for discussion of OEO's system.

Program impact evaluation is assessment of the overall effectiveness of a national program in meeting its objectives, or assessment of the relative effectiveness of two or more programs in meeting common objectives. The usual objective of program impact evaluation is to assist policy makers in reaching decisions on program funding levels or on possible redirection of a program. Program impact evaluation depends on the definition and measurement of appropriate *output variables* and on the use of appropriate *comparison groups*. Environmental and process data usually are not essential. The Westinghouse Learning Corporation-Ohio University study of the national Head Start program is an example of a program impact evaluation.

Program strategy evaluation is assessment of the relative effectiveness of different techniques used in a national program. The usual objective of program strategy evaluation is to inform program managers of the relative effectiveness of the different strategies or methods used by projects in the national program. Program strategy evaluation depends on definition and measurement of appropriate *environmental, input, process* and *output* variables selected on the basis of suitable analytic models. The Stanford Research Institute study of the national Follow Through program—an attempt to determine the relative effectiveness of several different approaches to primary education of disadvantaged children—is an example of a program strategy evaluation.

Project evaluation is assessment of the effectiveness of an individual project in achieving its stated objectives. This form of evaluation is required in many federal programs and is often carried out by the project itself. Project evaluation requires measurement of the important *output* variables as well as the use of appropriate *comparison groups*. A more feasible form of project evaluation simply compares project results with performance objectives or baseline conditions, omitting the use of comparison groups and therefore usually reducing the possibility of attributing effects to the treatments provided. Title I of the Elementary and Secondary Education Act, for example, requires evaluation of the thousands of local projects funded through Title I.

Project rating is assessment of the relative effectiveness of different local projects in achieving program objectives. The usual objective of project rating is to provide program managers with information on the relative success of local projects operating within a national program. In most cases, it will make sense to rate projects against one another only if they are operating in similar environments. Project rating depends on definition and measurement of *environmental* variables and relatively inexpensive *output* measures (e.g., measures of short-term impact). The Department of Health, Education and Welfare system for rating Work Experience and Training projects is an example of project rating.

These four types of evaluation can vary in the level of detail considered and in the level of decision-making affected. In addition, the relative importance and feasibility of these four types will vary from program to program and over time. In subsequent sections, the usefulness and feasibility of these four types of evaluation for any given program are discussed. It will be indicated when the federal government should conduct none, one, or more of these types of evaluation, depending on the program in question and its stage of development.

Evaluation Alternatives

In addition to the four types of evaluation just defined, this report also discusses two alternatives to evaluation of on-going programs—field experiments and experimental demonstrations.

Program strategy evaluation can be carried out in two ways. One is to study the natural variations in approach that may occur among different groups of projects in a national program. A second way is to introduce "planned variations" in approach for study in some systematic fashion. With "planned variation," we begin to move from evaluation of on-going operating programs to smaller-scale program experimentation. It is often advantageous, due to financial, methodological or practical constraints, to operate portions of a program or groups of demonstration projects in such a way as to systematically test different approaches. Two alternatives are recommended:

Field experiments with careful specification of treatment groups and control groups, control over input and process variables, and careful measurement of input, process and output variables.

Experimental demonstrations without control groups but with control over input and process variables and with careful measurement of input, process and output variables. Projects operate under an overall design which allows comparison of the relative effects of alternative treatments.

Evaluation-Related Activities

Monitoring, reporting systems and cost analysis are three evaluation-related activities that all have one thing in common, differentiating them from evaluation: they focus on program inputs.

Monitoring is the assessment of managerial and operational efficiency of programs or projects through periodic site visits and other management techniques. The usual objective of monitoring is to give program managers impressionistic data about how their projects are going, to see if they are being run efficiently, if they are following program guidelines, if they have competent staffs—in general, to do a management assessment of the soundness of individual projects.

Reporting Systems, which provide routine reporting from state or local level, are not evaluation but may furnish useful data on services provided, populations served and costs of providing services. In some cases, it may be justifiable to spend evaluation funds to defray state and local costs of providing such data, as well as follow-up data on specified samples of program or project participants, when the data are required to meet clearly specified evaluation needs.

Cost Analysis is a means of obtaining information for program managers on the cost of providing services through a program. Comparative analysis of costs by project, by groups of projects or by program is essential to good evaluation and is a valuable management tool in itself.

3. Administration of an Evaluation System

In a given year, a federal agency may expend several million dollars and considerable staff time on various types of evaluation activities. Regardless of the time and money involved, the overall effectiveness of federal evaluation depends on the competent execution of several key administrative tasks. To assist decisions affecting public programs, an adequate evaluation system must perform at least the following functions, each of which will be discussed in turn:

Definition of program objectives and output measures.
Development of evaluation work plans.
Design and execution of evaluation studies.
Dissemination and use of evaluation study findings.

DEFINITION OF PROGRAM OBJECTIVES

Most of the programs examined lacked adequately defined criteria of program effectiveness. This lack stems partially from the fact that the typical federal program has multiple objectives and partially from difficulties in defining objectives in measurable terms, particularly when the authorizing legislation is very general. But the widespread absence of evaluation criteria stems mainly from two things—the failure of program managers to think through their objectives, and the failure by evaluators to insist on the guidance they need to define evaluation criteria. The lack of clear administrative guidelines also reflects poor understanding of the relationship of program activities and ultimate goals.

The definitional problem is illustrated by the HEW Maternal and Child Health programs. The objectives range from the broad and general aims of grants "for maternal and child health services," to the detailed objectives of the maternity and infant care projects "to help reduce the incidence of mental retardation and other handicapping conditions caused by complications associated with child bearing and to help reduce infant and maternal mortality."[4]

For manpower programs, on the other hand, the objectives and effectiveness criteria are more obvious. Job Corps, for example, has established output measures for both the program and individual projects: the program is evaluated by the ex-corpsmen's subsequent increased earnings and reduced unemployment; the projects (Job Corps Centers) are measured in terms of retention rates and length of stay, which have been found to be closely related to post-Job Corps employability.

An agency may face one or all of these definitional problems in any program area. Recently enacted health programs are typical. The purpose of OEO's Neighborhood Health Centers program is to provide health care to the poor. However, as part of the Community Action Program, it also shares, as an additional goal, that of the whole poverty program: to focus all resources in a local strategy to eliminate poverty. Other programs are equally broad. The Comprehensive Health Planning and Public Health Services Act of 1966 (P.L. 89-749) and the Partnership for Health Act of 1967 (P.L. 90-174) ended the categorical type project grants directed toward specific diseases—tuberculosis, cancer, heart disease, V.D.—and stated the broad goal of "promoting and assuring the highest level of health attainable for every person, in an environment which contributes positively to healthful individual and family living . . ." The goal of the Medicaid program, similarly, is to make available by 1975 "high quality comprehensive medical care" to those of all ages unable to pay for it.

These programs aim at changes in the organization of the health delivery system and impact on the health status of the target group. Improved quality of life is a stated or implied goal in each.

---

4. Title V of the Social Security Act.

Specifying meaningful long-term and short-term output measures for such global programs is a formidable task. It involves an understanding of the relationship between health status, poverty, and the utilization of health services—but these links are by no means always clear. (Even if one cannot measure effects of health care programs on health status, it can be significant to measure the reaction of disparities in available medical services.)

Agency Role

The difficulty of stating objectives is more dramatic when viewed in its organizational setting. Consider, for example, the Department of Housing and Urban Development. The old Housing and Home Finance Agency, before and after its transformation into a Cabinet Department in 1966, constantly experienced major changes. While the omnibus housing acts of 1949, 1954, 1956, 1961, 1964 and 1968 are most often remembered and cited, the fact is that either the organization, responsibilities, policies or programs were altered in virtually every year since the federal government first made an in-depth commitment to play a role in housing and urban problems.

In most cases, the objectives of HUD's legislative enactments are stated in very broad, general terms, such as ". . .to remedy the unsafe and insanitary housing conditions. . .[of]. . .families of low income, in urban, rural, nonfarm and Indian areas, that are injurious to the health, safety, and morals of the citizens of the Nation."[5] There are exceptions. For example, the statements of purpose for the Model Cities program include several which are reasonably more precise. The law identifies intended beneficiaries in "slum and blighted areas" and includes such goals as "to expand housing, job, and income opportunities, . . .to reduce dependence on welfare payments, . . .to establish better access between homes and jobs." It should be ascertainable, over time, whether or not these contemplated changes have actually occurred.[6]

---

5. Sec. 1, U.S. Housing Act of 1937, amended, 42 U.S.C. 1401 *et seq.*

6. The Department of Housing and Urban Development has published a document ("Technical Assistance Bulletin No. 2: Measures of Living Quality in Model Neighborhoods") which has been used by local city demonstration agencies as a reference work when they developed the objectives for their

By far the largest HUD program is the urban renewal program, originally authorized by Title I of the Housing Act of 1949. It was unique in its extensive reliance on public funds for private as well as for public benefits. For the present and the predictable future, urban renewal expenditures are far greater than all the various subsidized housing programs combined. Debate on its merits or success aside, the impact of urban renewal on the urban scene is greater than that of other current activities of the department— even of the Model Cities program which affects a far smaller universe of communities and which is in a much earlier stage of development. The urban renewal program therefore would seem to be a prime candidate for a strong evaluation effort. In fact, the department has not carried out objective and useful evaluation to any considerable extent. A prime reason is that legislation does not require that urban renewal be evaluated. The Renewal Assistance Administration, moreover, faces problems common to other multi-objective agencies: (1) translating nebulous objectives into specific aims, (2) developing national objectives without unduly restricting local prerogatives, (3) finding suitable methodology, and (4) overcoming the high cost of collecting data. Despite extensive studies of urban renewal by non-government institutions, the development of methodology for urban renewal evaluation is still in the formative stage.

Role of Program Managers and Evaluators

In spite of the difficulties in defining evaluation criteria, much more can be done with the tools available today. Much of the blame for the present state of affairs must be placed with program managers for failure to be explicit about their objectives and with evaluators for failure to insist on the guidance they need to define evaluation criteria.

Clearly stated objectives are crucial to those demonstration grant programs that seek to test promising program approaches for possible adoption on a broad scale. In the Office of Education Follow Through program, for example, a number of promising approaches to education of disadvantaged children is being

---

model neighborhood programs. HUD required the cities to state objectives and to try to quantify objectives wherever possible.

tested.[7] The guidelines state that Follow Through is intended to
provide comprehensive services to facilitate the total development—not only academic achievement—of disadvantaged children
of primary school age, particularly those children who have had a
full year in Head Start or a similar program.

In an early evaluation of the program, predating its reorienta-
tion to a national experimental demonstration program, the
University of Pittsburgh was forced to extract Follow Through
program objectives from the individual project proposals (169). In
June 1968, Stanford Research Institute was funded to evaluate the
national Follow Through program and has faced much the same
problem. Not enough guidance has come from Office of Education personnel on the precise objectives and output measures of
major interest in the Follow Through evaluation effort.

After almost two years of the SRI national effort, it is clear that
the objectives of sponsors[8] of the different program models vary a
great deal. These sponsors and the national evaluation contractor
are both interested in broadening the output measures of the
national evaluation to include the objectives of the various program sponsors. There is no doubt that everyone in the Follow
Through program has the general objective of improving education
for disadvantaged children, but specific approaches vary so widely
that a good deal of effort is required even now to make explicit
(1) Follow Through's own educational achievement objectives,
(2) other objectives relating to individual students, (3) objectives
relating to changes in the behavior of teachers, and (4) objectives
involving changes in the entire school or school system in which

---

7. Follow Through offers school districts a "menu" of different curricula
for disadvantaged children in the early elementary grades. Participating school
districts opt for one of the models offered and in the course of the year
receive advice and counsel of consultants in implementing the approach
selected.

8. An important characteristic of the Follow Through program is the
fact that program sponsors have been employed to work with local school
districts providing training and supervision for up to 12 or 15 communities
each. The Follow Through sponsors, university-based, have been able to provide this technical assistance to a greater or lesser degree depending on when
the communities came into the Follow Through program and what size staff
the sponsors were able to bring on.

the Follow Through program is being introduced.[9] More attention should be given to agreement on what long-term results—in terms of child, teacher and institutional behavior—the Follow Through program is seeking by, say, 1972 or 1973.

Follow Through shows that, difficult as it may be, an evaluator can extract objectives from operations.[10] This is helpful in ensuring that relevant outputs are taken into account in the design of an evaluation study. Agency guidance to evaluators on what the program objectives are, however, is far more desirable than trying to find goals between the lines.

Positive and Negative Side Effects

Determining whether a program is meeting its objectives is not all the evaluator must measure. He also faces the additional task of estimating the important side effects caused by a program.

In the past, side effects have received little attention from program managers or policy makers. The effects of FHA insurance policies and practices on segregation, urban sprawl and the decline of the central cities, for example, went virtually unnoticed for years. Similarly, it came as somewhat of a surprise to many of those who managed public housing that their projects often seemed to magnify problems of delinquency and family disintegration. Only recently have the socially destructive aspects of public assistance programs been acknowledged. It is the task of managers

---

9. The Follow Through sponsors place great emphasis on institutional change as one of the main objectives of the Follow Through program. Some sponsors believe that, unless major changes take place in the schools, any gains resulting from Follow Through by the third grade would probably disappear by the sixth grade.

10. The empirical search for "operative goals" is not by any means unique to Follow Through. Consider the following statement from an evaluation study: "The goals and objectives of the Neighborhood Health Centers have not been formally outlined by the OEO in a way which leads logically into evaluation. However, from statements in the Official Guidelines of the need for the centers and the elements which each center is to contain, a formal outline of the program's hierarchy of objectives can be deduced." Madison (132).

and evaluators to assemble fair assessments of both positive and negative side effects.

Data Reporting Requirements

Even when realistic output measures are available, the gathering of program output data may not be easy or straightforward. In 1965, HEW's Office of Education formulated very clear objectives for the ESEA Title I program: statistically significant gains in pupil achievement, improvement of attitudes as measured by standard instruments, reduction in drop-outs, increased attendance rates and increased rates of post-high school education. However, the recurring problem of data reporting from the states was not solved. Because states lacked interest and incentive—and, in some cases, because they did not want to circulate information that they conceived to be damaging to themselves in some way—they did not send in the required data.

The only way local education agencies could have been forced to comply with reporting standards in the OE guidelines would have been to threaten them with loss of federal funds, a step that the Office of Education was not willing to take over the issue of data collection. Consequently HEW has not established national reporting criteria for the Title I program.

In the area of defining objectives, HEW has clarified the health and welfare aims of its family planning programs; HUD has suggested reasonable measures for many Model Cities program objectives; OEO requires community action agencies to identify local objectives in terms of national goals for community action and then to assess progress toward these local objectives when applying for grant renewal. Generally, however, program managers and policy makers can go much further toward specifying criteria by which program effectiveness can be measured.

At the beginning of a program, evaluators should be responsible for assisting program managers and policy makers in defining these criteria—whenever possible, in terms that permit measurement. Ideally, agency staffs should get clear statements of desired program outputs incorporated into the authorizing legislation itself.

RECOMMENDATIONS—DEFINING PROGRAM OBJECTIVES

1. Agency heads should direct their evaluation staffs to work with program managers and policy makers to define the multiple criteria by which each major program is to be judged. To the extent possible, criteria should be defined in terms that permit measurement of program outputs and also of potential positive or negative effects on other public objectives.

2. Staff at program, agency and Budget Bureau levels should review criteria for evaluation of important programs to ensure that the objectives of Congress, policy makers and program administrators are addressed. Related programs generally should be evaluated according to common output measures to facilitate inter-program comparisons.

3. Program objectives and the choice of evaluation criteria should be determined by agency and program staffs rather than by outside contractors.

4. Statements of desired program results should be incorporated in authorizing legislation.

5. Local project managers should be encouraged to state, and to periodically measure their progress toward, specific objectives.

6. Evaluation staff at agency and operating levels should plan and carry out basic research to determine the adequacy of existing output measures.

DEVELOPING WORK PLANS

With few exceptions, federal agencies have had no adequate work plans for evaluating their major social programs.

The limited evaluation funds available have been spent without establishment of priorities among possible studies. The result is that important answerable questions about the effectiveness of a program were often left unanswered when the time came to review the program and decide its future.

The lack of evaluation work plans often resulted in haphazard letting of unrelated contracts to evaluate the same program. Contractors designed their own studies, formulated their own questions and naturally produced data and findings that were noncomparable with each other.

Again, some progress has been made: OEO's Office of Planning, Research and Evaluation has developed a plan for major program impact evaluation studies. The DOL Manpower Administration Office of Evaluation is shifting its spending from monitoring to program impact and program strategy evaluations. HEW has recently developed a plan for evaluation of its education programs. And HUD's Model Cities Administration produced a plan for evaluation of the Model Cities program, although portions of the plan still awaited approval at the departmental level.

First attempts at developing work plans resulted, for the most part, in listings of proposed studies developed without any overall rationale or strategy. But a work plan should be comprehensive and systematic. It should be a multi-year plan, updated at the beginning of each year to set evaluation priorities based on careful analysis of the following factors: (a) identification of high priority policy questions, (b) methodological feasibility of responding to these questions, (c) practicability of implementing the study design, (d) the cost, and (e) the in-house staff required.

Best Work Plans Found in OEO

OEO has gone farthest in developing agency-level evaluation work plans. For program impact evaluations, OEO has both a multi-year plan and a general evaluation strategy, designed to answer four basic questions about each OEO program (29):

> Does the program reasonably address the needs of those towards whom it is aimed?
>
> To what extent does it reach the intended population?
>
> How successfully is it achieving its objectives?
>
> How does its cost compare with the value of its benefits?

Table 1 shows a matrix used by OEO in 1968 to guide the initial development of program impact evaluation plans. The matrix serves as a general model for the overall evaluation of anti-poverty programs; its use for agency planning and programing is explained in the note on the same page. There are recognized limitations to this approach but, everything considered, this is a

Table 1. Paradigm for OEO Program Impact Evaluations[a]

Evaluation Data	Job Corps	VISTA	Organization-Coordination Functions	Anti-Poverty Programs[b] — Community Action Programs — Service Programs						Delegated Programs	Non-OEO Project
				Legal Services	Head Start	Follow Through	Upward Bound	Health Services	Others		
A. Universe of need (demand)											
B. Program reach											
C. Program coverage (A/B)											
D. Program cost											
E. Cost per person reached (D/B)											
F. Cost of total coverage (E) x (A)[c]											
G. Measures of program effectiveness: 1. Immediate objectives 2. Poverty reduction (budget)											
H. Benefit-cost ratio (G/D)											

37

[a] John Evans explained the use of the matrix as follows: "Going down the left-hand Evaluation Data column from A through H will indicate how the completed paradigm would be useful in overall agency planning and programming. With extensive and dependable data for each program on universe of need (A) and program reach (B), we can calculate and compare progress on the extent to which they are reaching their target populations (C). A solid figure on program coverage (C) would be very useful in planning and budgeting both within a given program and across the total array of OEO programs. Bringing together for all programs the information on their total costs (D) (on which we have good data) and information on the number of people they reach (B) (on which we don't) would allow us to compute, and compare programs on, the cost per person reached (E). With information on program costs (D), the total universe of need (A), and the present program reach (B), we could determine for each program what the cost of total coverage would be and how much of an increment over present budget outlays this would require (F)" (29, p. 233).

[b] A number of the programs listed have since been delegated to the Departments of Labor and of Health, Education, and Welfare.

[c] A correct computation would not be this simple but would take into account the marginal cost required to expand programs at different levels.

useful strategy to assist in the development of program impact evaluation.

OEO has undertaken, or plans to undertake, program impact evaluations of Head Start, Upward Bound, the Community Action Program, Family Planning, Neighborhood Health Centers, and the Legal Services Programs. OEO is also directing a joint OEO-DOL three-year longitudinal comparative evaluation of five manpower training programs—Job Corps, Neighborhood Youth Corps out-of-school programs, MDTA institutional programs, New Careers, and Job Opportunities in the Business Sector (JOBS). This is an impressive effort, whether viewed alone or in comparison with the scope of program impact evaluations in other agencies.

OEO has not been as successful in developing work plans for program strategy evaluations, nor has OEO been able to coordinate the various types of evaluation and evaluation-related activities (field experiments, reporting systems, monitoring, etc.). The practice has been for the Office of the Director to request annual evaluation work plans from the different program evaluation staffs. The fiscal year 1969 and 1970 plans prepared by OEO reflected those submitted by program offices: listings of planned and on-going studies, with no indication of either evaluation strategy or the relationships of studies to operational problems and issues. One study (117) of OEO was critical of this process:

> A request was sent from the Office of the Director to the program offices for information on future evaluations. The program offices typically responded with lists of projects currently underway, under contract, or in some way envisioned for the future. From such responses, the RPP&E Evaluation Division prepared a summary plan.... The summary evaluation plan has the same features as the program office plans that it summarizes—it is a listing of future evaluation projects. Rather than a listing of envisioned evaluation projects, an OEO evaluation plan should be a coordinated, overall presentation of the OEO strategy for evaluation. It would be useful for this strategy to start with a presentation of all of the operating programs. This would be followed by the planned evaluation efforts for each operating program. In this way, the overall distribution and levels of OEO evaluation efforts can be seen as they relate to the operating programs. In addition, the evaluation plans and operating programs should be time phased to show the evaluation strategy for discrete future time periods (117, p. 233).

Job Corps was singled out in the same report as the one OEO program having a plan resembling a time-phased overall strategy. The fiscal year 1969 plan described research and evaluation projects relating to the various operational Job Corps program components (recruitment, screening, assignment, center process, placement, and follow-up).

Other Agency Efforts

The above critique of OEO's annual evaluation plan also applies to the efforts of HEW and DOL (as it no doubt would to the early work plans in almost any agency). Generally, work plans either do not exist or are simply lists of studies lacking an overall rationale or strategy.

At HEW, for example, the Assistant Secretary for Planning and Evaluation (ASPE) was given responsibility late in 1967 for coordinating department-wide efforts to improve HEW program evaluation. The other responsibilities of ASPE were so pressing that ASPE had not been able to coordinate and give directions to evaluation efforts. Only by late 1969 was ASPE able to establish a system for planning, funding, and executing department-level evaluation studies and for closer review of evaluation activities in HEW agencies and bureaus. For example, the Office of Education prepared, with the approval and assistance of the Office of the Secretary of HEW, a fiscal year 1970 evaluation work plan.

During this same recent period, the Office of the Secretary of Labor began preparation of the first DOL evaluation plan, while the Manpower Administration made great strides in both design of important individual evaluation studies and in strategic planning for evaluation and the use of evaluation studies.

The Office of the Secretary of Housing and Urban Development, on the other hand, continued to review individual evaluation studies planned at operating levels but has not developed the capability for the conducting or strategic planning of department-wide evaluation efforts. Apart from a few relatively limited and unrepeated studies, there was no example of a substantial, on-going HUD program evaluation effort until the decision to launch a major effort in connection with Model Cities. HUD's

Model Cities Administration has produced an evaluation plan that is still awaiting approval at departmental level.

Cost of Failure to Plan

Recent experience has shown the haphazard results of unplanned and uncoordinated evaluation. In the past few years the federal government has spent a substantial amount of money on evaluation of social programs without getting much in return.[11] After five years of operating and evaluating compensatory education programs, such as ESEA Title I and Head Start, we are still unable to say with confidence what works and what doesn't. We have not even gone very far in formulating the critical policy and program issues. The result of unplanned evaluation programs has been a proliferation of non-comparable, poorly designed studies with little or no policy relevance.

RECOMMENDATIONS–DEVELOPING WORK PLANS

7. Approved evaluation plans should be required at the beginning of each fiscal year as a condition for authority to spend evaluation funds. The plans should be revised in the middle of each fiscal year to conform with budgets actually appropriated.

8. Evaluation work plans should cover a two- to three-year period and should specify (a) significant questions to be answered on the effectiveness of major national programs, program strategies and local projects, (b) estimated dates by which answers are needed for legislative, budgetary and policy reviews, (c) general types of evaluations planned and under way, (d) specific questions each study is designed to answer, (e) estimated cost of each study, (f) in-house staff and funds available for the studies, (g) agency priorities among studies listed, and (h) important questions that will *not* be addressed in the current work plan.

9. To help comply with 8(c), agencies should use this checklist to note how much of the following evaluation and evaluation-related activities are required for each major program or group of related

---

11. For the fifteen programs examined in this study, 1969 evaluation expenditures were approximately $17 million.

programs: (a) national program impact evaluation, (b) program strategy evaluation, (c) field experiments and experimental demonstrations, (d) project rating, (e) local project evaluation, (f) monitoring, routine reporting and cost analysis, and (g) development and demonstration of evaluation methodology.

10. Since evaluations are likely to be costly while agency staff and funds are limited, proposed studies should be reviewed searchingly for methodological feasibility, probable cost in relation to the probable value of findings, comparability with related evaluations, usefulness relative to other proposed studies and appropriateness of the assignment of responsibility for the evaluations. (See Chapter 6, especially "Feasibility," and Chapter 4 for organizational responsibilities.) For example, manpower programs stand out as good candidates for evaluation because the programs are important, policy decisions are required, and reliable short-term and medium-term output measures are available. To carry this a step further, highest priority for the manpower programs examined should be given to project rating and program strategy evaluation, combined with field experiments and experimental demonstrations to learn what program strategies and components are most effective.

11. Good work plans require widespread involvement. An overall administration evaluation plan should be prepared by the Budget Bureau program evaluation staff with inputs from the White House, Urban Affairs Council, BOB examining divisions and the agencies. Agency work plans should be prepared by agency-level evaluation staff with inputs from policy makers, program planners, budget staffs, program managers and operating-level evaluation staffs.

12. Attention should be paid to the desirability of combining two or more proposed studies or of joining formal evaluation with more traditional management or fiscal audit activities.

13. Work plans usually should not include unsolicited evaluation proposals as they tend to be drawn up without detailed knowledge of program objectives or priority policy questions.

14. Work plans prepared at operating bureau and program level should be reviewed by the agency to make certain proposed studies will meet agency needs; similarly, agency plans should be reviewed by the Bureau of the Budget to assure evaluations that can serve White House and Budget Bureau needs.

DESIGN AND EXECUTION OF STUDIES

Because the evaluation staffs in most federal agencies are small, there is a tendency for agencies to turn over to outside organizations as much of the evaluation process as possible. Unless given clear direction and careful monitoring, however, contractors naturally tend to design studies in accord with their own interests but which may be far afield from the main policy-related questions that need to be addressed. Also, contractors have a tendency to overstate in their initial proposals what their studies realistically can accomplish.

It thus became evident that one of the basic deficiencies in the contracting process was the lack of evaluators *within* the agencies having the skill and the time to design studies, prepare clear Requests for Proposals (RFPs), assess the validity of proposals, and work closely with the contractors during the course of their studies.

Owing to the large staff investment required to monitor outside contractors, agencies should consider placing more emphasis on obtaining their own staff to conduct in-house evaluations. In such cases, contractors should be used primarily for clearly specified subtasks. Whether large or limited use is made of outside help for evaluations, agency in-house evaluation staffs can improve the contracting process by providing incentives for exemplary performance.

Contract Hazards

OEO offers two examples—Head Start and the Community Action Program—of the "wrong studies" or "non-studies" that are not relevant to policy decisions or that cannot be generalized with any confidence.[12]

With a staff of only one to two professionals to handle $3 million per year in evaluation contracts, OEO's Head Start Office relied heavily on consultant staff, independent contractors, and

---

12. Because OEO has gone farther than other agencies in developing evaluation, it often offers the best examples of what can go wrong.

regional Evaluation and Research Centers for the design of evaluation studies and for the implementation of data collection.[13] For the most part, coordination of these efforts was impossible. OEO reviewed the best of the resulting impact studies and found them weak in design and method and of little operational usefulness (39, 179). OEO's Evaluation Division concluded that Head Start evaluation efforts would have been more productive with a few large-scale, well-designed studies. These could have been administered more effectively.

In contrast, OEO's central Evaluation Division has had five to six professionals to administer $3 million in evaluation funds. This division has purposely limited the number of studies under way to allow for careful planning and monitoring of each evaluation study by in-house staff. The OEO Evaluation Division put the required in-house staff effort into the recent Westinghouse evaluation (174) of the Head Start program, for example.

Before OEO's central Evaluation Division assumed responsibility for program impact evaluation, the CAP program office had funded one program impact study of its own, "A Comprehensive Evaluation of Eight Community Action Programs," at a total cost of over $1.6 million. This study was started early in 1967 as an "independently conducted, comprehensive, three-year evaluation of all phases of the community action programs in eight different rural and urban localities." Each of the eight contractors was given a free hand in choosing methodology and approach. Without any overall design or framework, coordination and comparison became very difficult if not impossible. The results to date have been unsatisfactory. The program office has been criticized for not defining its evaluation objectives nor developing coordinated approaches with the contractors. In the past year, the emphasis on evaluation in the CAP program office has turned toward more comprehensive, large-sample studies, with greater in-house supervision.

---

13. Since 1966, OEO has supported 13 university-based Evaluation and Research Centers. They were to undertake a basic research program and collect data for a nationwide evaluation of Head Start. Recently, their role in evaluation has been terminated.

Requests for Proposals

Agencies will have to put far greater resources into preparation of the work statements for evaluation studies—in particular, Requests for Proposals. These RFPs should state clearly the purpose of the proposed study, the policy and operational questions to be addressed, general methodology appropriate for answering the questions, measures of effectiveness to be included, and the state of present knowledge about the effectiveness of the programs and related programs. Unsolicited evaluation proposals which agency staff have had no hand in designing should be carefully reviewed and discouraged unless they clearly serve the agency's evaluation needs.

The RFPs issued in fiscal year 1969 by the Community Action Program Evaluation Branch were of high quality, well above average for a federal agency. Although they varied widely, generally they contained the following essential elements:

> Background of the project or procedure to be studied. Purpose of the evaluation clarified with lists of questions to be answered and statement of how findings were to be used. Expected evaluation products, along with the procedures or mechanics for obtaining them.

> Design of the overall evaluation. (In one case, a field-tested design was presented; in other cases, data collection and sampling requirements were partially specified.) Results of past studies, and their relation to the present effort. Comparisons with similar past evaluations were requested.

In some cases, the RFP outlined a two-phased contract—the first for the evaluation, the second for providing training and technical assistance to the regional offices, state economic opportunity offices, Community Action Program training centers and selected community action agencies and other local organizations.

Contract Monitoring

Rarely can it be said that evaluation offices *do* evaluations; for the most part they design and monitor contracts for evaluation studies. When contractors do not begin with a clear idea of what is being evaluated, proposals understandably fail to reflect technically sound design or methodology. The typical RFP procurement has led to disproportionate investments of time, effort and money merely to acquaint the contractors with the nature of the problem—so much so, in fact, that resources not infrequently were exhausted during this stage, and studies became passably competent restatements of problems, together with findings that they deserved further study.[14]

Because contractors tend to oversell what they can accomplish, they often are paid more for writing proposals than for doing evaluations. Alternative contracting mechanisms, therefore, should be tested. These should include incentives or penalties to strengthen the evaluation office's hand in contract monitoring. Some incentive mechanisms that might be considered are:

(a) Planning Grants. After the RFP is issued, a few contractors would be selected to receive grants to write operational proposals. Then the best of these would be selected for the final design.

(b) Time Phasing of Payments. To control cost overruns, the contractor would submit cost data incrementally and be paid in phases.

(c) Time Phasing of Work Loads. An evaluation of twenty health centers, for example, would be broken into two phases—evaluation of five, then evaluation of the remaining fifteen. The second phase would not be approved unless the agency was satisfied with the first.

RECOMMENDATIONS–DESIGN AND EXECUTION OF STUDIES

15. Far greater resources should be devoted to preparation of work statements for evaluation studies, and particularly for Requests for Proposals (RFPs). These statements should specify policy and operational questions to be answered, effectiveness measures to be used, general methodologies that appear appropriate, what is already known about the performance of programs being examined (and of related programs), and the intended use of the findings.

---

14. A disproportionate investment of time can easily go into selecting the contractors. There are an estimated 300 firms qualified to receive RFP's from OEO, for example. It isn't necessary to inform all contractors of proposed studies as long as adequate competition is assured. However, all proposals received must be considered, and the word does get around.

16. While execution of studies frequently may be handled by contractors, study designs and evaluation criteria generally should be
determined by agency and program staff.

Studies Without Impact

Evaluation is a decision-making tool. Its success or failure must be
measured, therefore, in terms of its impact on changing program
policies and resource allocations. As Williams and Evans have
written, "In thinking about the development of evaluations, it
must be remembered that after a decision is reached, the further
hurdle remains of translating the decision into effective operating
policy so as to improve the performance of the agency's programs.
Those who plan evaluations need to be sensitive to an agency's
administrative structure through which policy decisions are implemented for, in the final analysis, *the test of the effectiveness of
outcome data is its impact on implemented policy*" (emphasis
added) (179, p. 453). By this standard, there is a dearth of successful evaluation studies.

The recent literature is unanimous in announcing the general
failure of evaluation to affect decision making in a significant
way.[15]

---

15. Clarence C. Sherwood, National Conference on Social Welfare,
Chicago, June 1966: "It must be admitted that to date very limited results
have been produced by controlled scientific evaluation of action programs."
Egon Guba's version of the schoolman's definition of evaluation (quoted by
Daniel Stufflebeam in *Evaluation as Enlightenment for Decision-Making*,
Ohio State University, College of Education Evaluation Center, 1968): "Evaluation is something required from on high that takes time and pain to produce but which has very little significance for action." Carol Weiss in a paper
presented at the American Sociological Association, Miami Beach, Sept. 1,
1966: "The basic rationale for evaluation is that it provides information for
action. Its primary justification is that it contributes to the rationalization of
decision-making. Although it can serve such other functions as knowledge-
building and theory testing, unless it gains serious hearing when program
decisions are made, it fails in its major purpose. The record to date appears to
be an indifferent one." Grosse et al. in the GAO report on OEO: "Evaluation
efforts have absorbed a good deal of resources at OEO, particularly when
compared with the evaluation efforts of other agencies. What has been ob-

While most observers acknowledge the low impact of current evaluation studies, others go on to question the expectations most analysts hold for achieving measurable impact. The RMC study of OEO evaluation sounded the following pessimistic note:

> The broader studies tend to present the issue of resource allocation crudely in the form of large indivisible alternatives, that, if not indigestible, may at least prove unpalatable. One may find a favorable benefit-cost estimate being used to support requests for increased program appropriations or in opposition to proposed cuts, but there is little reason to suppose that modest benefit-cost ratios (or even negative ones) lead to formal requests by program managers for program elimination or cut-back. Where such major changes in resource allocation do occur, the mechanism appears much more complex, since it would appear to involve not only the upper reaches of the Executive Branch, including the Bureau of the Budget, but also the participation of Congress. In this process, the precise role of a particular evaluation project becomes somewhat obscure, particularly in view of the likelihood that the adequacy or accuracy of the evaluation itself may be brought into question and that other considerations will also enter the decision process.
>
> In the case of more narrowly focused operations-oriented studies, the responsibility for related policy decisions (or lack of them) may be less diffuse (that is, easier to fix at a given level of program management), and the links between findings and impact may be more identifiable in some situations. The effects of such decisions taken singly, however, tend to be relatively small in terms of overall program structure. Even considered in the aggregate, most evaluation work of this kind does not call for major changes from present practice. Hence significant effects on program policy and resource allocation will occur mainly as a gradual shift of emphasis on technique as the consequences of relatively small decisions accumulate. Here again, then, the link between specific evaluation activities and specific changes in programs becomes obscure (118, pp. 41-42).

---

tained for this expense? In any concrete sense, the answer must be very little" (118, p. 23). Steffen Graae in an OEO internal paper: "Of all the issues raised in the course of this survey, utilization of findings was the hardest to pin down. Lack of centralized records, turnover of personnel, and limited access to field personnel rendered a systematic approach to this question impractical within the time permitted. However, this in itself would seem to suggest that utilization can only have been low" (39).

Some Influence Felt

Evaluations are not intended to render decision making a mechanical process, even if they were comprehensive or sophisticated enough to be used in that fashion. The need is not for studies that tell what to decide, but rather for studies that provide information useful to policy and program decision makers. In this respect, this investigation found the same absence of successful evaluations noted by other authors. OEO, where the most extensive evaluations had been done, was the most likely place to look for relationships between findings and program changes, but only a few cases of studies that have had an impact on policy or operations were found. The Westinghouse study of Head Start received much publicity and became a center of controversy (174). The evaluation was one of several factors influencing the direction of the program. It is difficult to weigh its specific impact. Before publication, the Bureau of the Budget exerted pressure on Head Start to devote about $10 million of Head Start funds for program experimentation designed to identify "best" approaches to early childhood education. It renewed this pressure after publication. However the Head Start office had already agreed to proceed with such an effort based on the "planned variation" approach used in the Office of Education Follow Through program. Those involved at OEO with planning and carrying out the study have made the following realistic comment on the role evaluation should and did play (179, p. 130):

> Thus, the study pushes policy-making toward certain decisions, particularly those involving within-program tradeoffs—more experimentation and more full-year projects in place of summer projects. Yet, and this would be true no matter how good the study was, the evidence is not a sufficient condition for major program-decisions. The last statement holds even for the within-program choices (tradeoffs, but not overall cutbacks) and takes on greater cogency when one seeks implications for decisions concerning the need for more, or fewer resources. The evaluative evidence must be considered in the light of other pieces of information and various highly important political judgments. For example: How deleterious would a program cutback be for program morale, or for our commitment to increase the outlays going to the disadvantaged for education? Surely, no reasonable person would claim the evaluative

evidence alone is sufficient. Rather, such choices ought to be political, in the broad sense of that term, with credible evaluative data—a commodity heretofore in short supply—being considered as one of the inputs in the choice process.

The highly acclaimed Job Corps cost/benefit and follow-up studies (11, 47, 164) were subjected to various interpretations within the Executive Branch during the 1969 congressional hearings. It is difficult to weigh the impact of evaluation findings on the changes and cutbacks in this politically unpopular program.

An illustration of evaluation informing policy makers is found in HEW. The generally negative findings of federal, state and local evaluation of the Title I elementary and secondary education program suggest that this program is not effectively improving the educational achievement of disadvantaged children. The current experimental demonstration program to test more promising approaches through the re-oriented Follow Through program directly results from perceptions stemming from Title I evaluations.

There are several examples of program component evaluations having affected Community Action Program policy. Resources were added to the CAP housing development corporations when studies showed that these corporations were succeeding in providing low-income housing. Evaluations of summer youth programs and neighborhood centers have resulted in substantial changes in policy guidelines.

However, these stand out as special cases. As a rule it is difficult to see any relationship between evaluation and policy making within CAP, which had no functional system to ensure utilization of results. So inadequate was CAP on this score that its evaluation staff was unable even to catalog and critique the evaluation studies contracted by the CAP program offices or to keep track of whether these studies had been used by program officers or project managers.[16] Most other evaluation staffs in the federal government experienced similar difficulty in documenting the use of completed evaluation studies at agency, program management, regional office, state and local levels.

---

16. See RFP No. 9180, "Assessment of CAP Evaluation Activities and a Design for the Dissemination of Relevant Evaluation Data and Findings to OEO and CAA's," dated May 26, 1969.

Major Roadblocks

There are four basic reasons for low utilization of evaluations:

Organizational inertia. Organizations tend to resist change whereas evaluation usually implies change.

Methodological weakness. Policy makers properly distrust the results of poorly done studies and rely instead on their own experiences or instincts.

Design irrelevance. Too many studies bear little or no relationship to the critical program and policy issues.

Lack of dissemination. The relevant decision makers are not shown or briefed on the results of useful studies.

Organizational inertia will always exist in one form or another, but the other three reasons that evaluations lack much impact are far from inherent in the situation. Existing methods *are* adequate for the evaluation of most social programs. The critical policy issues are *not* beyond conceptualization and design capability. Evaluation *can* be kept relevant if those carrying it out possess knowledge of the program, the policies shaping the program, and the organizational and administrative structure of the program, including the connections between the agency and implementation in the field.

Since a great many federal policy decisions on existing programs revolve around preparation of the annual budget, the evaluation function should be well represented in the budget preparation system. This has been accomplished, for example, in the Office of Economic Opportunity, where the OEO assistant director for planning, research and evaluation is responsible for preparation of the OEO budget, and in the Department of Housing and Urban Development, where the deputy under secretary for policy analysis and program evaluation is a principal member of the HUD budget review committee. The new Office of Education-Office of Planning, Research, and Evaluation could have similar impact on the Office of Education decision-making process.[17]

---

17. This OE office is intended also to promote public dissemination of results of research and demonstration programs being carried out by OE and by other educational institutions.

To keep decision makers at federal, regional office, state and local levels informed of evaluation findings, each agency should create a clearinghouse of agency work plans and completed evaluation studies. A valuable but often neglected function is preparation of brief summaries and critical reviews of significant evaluation studies, since such summaries may be all that decision makers will find time to read. The Manpower Administration of the Department of Labor has a formal system to abstract evaluation studies, bring them to the attention of program managers and policy makers, and follow up to see what results are achieved. Evaluation staffs should be held responsible for the active dissemination of significant evaluation findings to policy makers and program managers through printed materials, briefings and offers of technical assistance.

RECOMMENDATIONS–DISSEMINATION AND USE OF STUDIES

17. Because relevant studies are more likely to be useful and used, agency evaluation staffs should ensure that work plans reflect the needs of budget and program planning staffs and of program managers.

18. Each agency and the Bureau of the Budget should develop a system so that the results of evaluations—whether programs are achieving their objectives and how related programs compare—will be considered in the budget preparation and legislative processes.

19. Operating bureau chiefs and program managers should use evaluation evidence, such as the relative success of different projects or strategies, in the program management process.

20. Agency evaluation staffs should develop informal systems for bringing significant evaluation findings to decision makers when results become available and again at appropriate decision points.

21. Evaluation staffs should establish formal systems to disseminate evaluation results through printed materials, briefings, offers of technical assistance and direct memos to policy makers and program managers. Regular follow-up should be part of the dissemination process.

22. A clearinghouse of evaluation work plans, significant completed studies, brief summaries and critical reviews of studies should be developed by evaluation staff at agency or operating program level to assist in bringing important findings to the attention of decision makers at all levels of government.

4. *Organizational Relationships and Responsibilities*

The critical administrative evaluation tasks—definition of program objectives, development of evaluation work plans, design and execution of evaluation studies, and utilization of evaluation findings—were identified in Chapter 3. Responsibility for execution of these tasks now needs to be assigned, especially since it was found that the current inadequate execution of these tasks was due in large part to the haphazard organization of federal evaluation activities.

A discussion of federal evaluation policy is complicated by two related factors. Evaluation serves several masters, namely, the President, the Congress, federal agencies and, in many programs, state and local governments. Moreover, it supports two types of decisions: those directed to broad policy questions, such as choice of programs and budget levels, and those focused on program improvement. These two types of decisions imply a natural division of evaluation responsibilities between policy makers and program managers. This division will be blurred in practice, but it is useful both for removing bureaucratic obstacles to evaluation and for improving the objectivity of evaluation studies. The critical tasks of coordinating and institutionalizing evaluation, then, are to specify (a) who will decide what questions are to be asked about what programs or policies and (b) who will be given the responsibility and resources for carrying out the evaluation tasks.

Evaluation means different things to different levels of the government. Because Congress and the Bureau of the Budget deal with all functional program areas (health, education, employment and so forth), evaluation is useful at these top levels to help in deciding what programs to emphasize and how to divide the national budget. Federal agencies, with jurisdiction over specific program areas, need evaluation to help justify their budget requests and to aid in efficient allocation of resources. Program managers need evaluation to help in program control—day-to-day management decisions—and in internal program policy making. The project manager needs evaluative data to help him plan, define goals, set priorities and assess his project direction and progress.

The level at which evaluation is carried out, therefore, is crucial. It makes obvious sense to place the responsibility for the various types of evaluation at the levels appropriate to the decisions which the evaluation is to assist. No program manager should be expected to evaluate the worth of his program, for example, nor should a member of the program manager's staff be put in the position of having to criticize his boss. Conversely, an evaluation should be placed at the level that can best carry it through and implement its findings.

This chapter considers the organization of the evaluation process at various levels of government and recommends a general structure designed to facilitate the development, administration and utilization of evaluation studies.

CONGRESS

The low level of evaluation activity in federal agencies relates directly to the absence of specific program objectives in most legislation. Also, there has not been much strong congressional demand for evaluation.

Yet, of the little evaluation that has been done, most has been in response to congressional requirements. In the past few years, Congress has begun to press strongly for evaluation of certain major programs, often incorporating requirements for program evaluation into the authorizing legislation, and has in a number of cases made available the personnel and financial resources necessary to accomplish the required evaluations.

OEO Legislation. An example of just how far Congress can go toward legislatively specifying evaluation is contained in the 1967 amendments to the Economic Opportunity Act.[18] The amendments

---

18. Discussed further in Chapter 5, page 77 ff.

emphasized the need for careful evaluation of all OEO programs. Title II, the community action programs, received close attention. Section 201(a) notes the role of evaluation in resource allocation:

> Its [Title II's] specific purposes are to promote ... the greater use, subject to adequate evaluation, of new types of services and innovative approaches in attacking causes of poverty, so as to develop increasingly effective methods of employing available resources. . . .

Section 212(b) requires that the community action agencies adopt a systematic approach to program planning, operation and evaluation. Section 223 calls for evaluation of all Title II programs under standards developed and published by the Director, with the results to be considered in deciding whether to renew assistance:

> Sec. 223. (a) The Director shall provide for the continuing evaluation of programs under this title, including their effectiveness in achieving stated goals, their impact on related programs, and their structure and mechanisms for the delivery of services and including, where appropriate, comparisons with proper control groups composed of persons who have not participated in such programs. . . .
>
> (b) The Director shall develop and publish standards for evaluation of program effectiveness in achieving the objectives of this title. Such standards shall be considered in deciding whether to renew or supplement financial assistance provided by sections 221, 222, 230, and 231. . . .

Section 223 also calls upon the director to evaluate the impact of the "Green Amendment":

> (c) The Director shall provide by contract for the conduct of an independent study and evaluation of the action taken under sections 210 and 211 of this Act and the effects thereof. . . .

The 1967 amendments were quite explicit in their requirements for evaluation of Job Corps. Section 113 of the Act requires both follow-up studies on terminees and thorough cost-benefit analysis of the Job Corps program:

> Sec. 113. (a) The Director shall provide for the careful and systematic evaluation of the Job Corps program, directly or by contracting for independent evaluations, with a view to measuring specific benefits, so

far as practicable, and providing information needed to assess the effectiveness of program procedures, policies and methods of operation. In particular, this evaluation shall seek to determine the costs and benefits resulting from the use of residential as opposed to nonresidential facilities, from the use of facilities combining residential and nonresidential components, from the use of centers with large as opposed to small enrollments and from the use of different types of program sponsors, including public agencies, institutions of higher education, boards of education, and private corporations. The evaluation shall also include comparisons with proper control groups composed of persons who have not participated in the program. . . . He shall also secure, to the extent feasible, similar information directly from enrollees at appropriate intervals following their completion of the Job Corps program. The results of such evaluation shall be published and shall be summarized in the report required by section 608.

The 1967 amendments then called for an independent evaluation by directing the Comptroller General (GAO) to investigate and evaluate OEO programs and activities in order to determine:

(1) the efficiency of the administration of such programs and activities by the Office of Economic Opportunity . . . .

(2) the extent to which such programs and activities achieve the objectives set forth in the relevant part or title of the Economic Opportunity Act of 1964.

Need for facts. Increasingly, Congress wants to know if federal programs are contributing to solutions of problems and if they are worth the money being spent on them. This attitude is reflected, for example, in the remarks of Senator Winston L. Prouty during a hearing on poverty programs:

Year after year we sit and listen to this. If you don't have the facts, tell us so, and if you do have them, present them for our consideration. In that way, you will do more to implement this program and so will this committee. We have to have more information to evaluate the programs and justify them to our colleagues on the Senate floor. That is one of the greatest weaknesses I perceive year after year (168, p. 2800).

In order to answer these questions, Congress is beginning to make larger sums of money available for sustained evaluation efforts in a number of key program areas including health, education, job training and model cities. Congress has authorized or earmarked funds for evaluation in several pieces of legislation, including the Child Health Act of 1967, the Elementary and Secondary Education Amendments of 1967, the Partnership for Health Amendments of 1967, and the Vocational Rehabilitation Amendments of 1968. For other programs, including those authorized under the Economic Opportunity Act and the Demonstration Cities and Metropolitan Development Act, evaluation funds have been made available by administrative earmarking or through use of agency research funds.

Congress is giving limited but increasing evaluation responsibilities to the General Accounting Office. GAO in 1968 and 1969 moved from major emphasis on program/project monitoring to accomplishment of a limited number of national program impact evaluations. GAO intended to perform program strategy evaluation as well (164).

Aside from requiring evaluation studies, the desirability of a stronger congressional role in policy analysis was recently examined by Congress itself. After hearings and studies, the Joint Economic Committee's Subcommittee on Economy in Government reported (147, p. 13):

> The relationship of the executive and legislative branches pertaining to the use of executive analysis and evaluation documents is a serious problem. More serious, however, is the failure of the Congress to provide itself with an analytical capability. Currently, the Congress has neither an adequate capability to interpret or evaluate studies done by the executive and those outside of government nor the necessary capacity to undertake policy analysis of its own.

This subcommittee report went on to recommend that, "to increase the effectiveness with which it reviews and scrutinizes program and appropriations decisions," Congress should establish an Office of Economic Evaluation and Analysis to provide Congress with "objective and independent program studies and policy analyses."

Congressional committees often have been singled out as having a low capability to deal with and use analyses. The following recommendation was offered by one analyst as a means of strengthening the hand of Congress in dealing with federal agencies on matters of policy analysis and evaluation:

A Congress that takes seriously its policy role should be encouraged to contract for policy analysis that would stress different views of what the critical questions are in a particular area of policy. Each major committee or subcommittee should be encouraged to hire a man trained in policy analysis for a limited period, perhaps two years. His task would be to solicit policy studies, evaluate presentations made by government agencies, and keep congressmen informed about what are considered the important questions (146, pp. 849-850).

RECOMMENDATIONS–ROLE OF CONGRESS

Congress plays an important role in establishing and shaping a federal evaluation system and can improve the current situation in several ways.

23. *Specifying Objectives.* Congress should include in each major piece of social legislation a statement of purpose in such a form as to facilitate evaluation of the resulting program activity. When possible, Congress should take this one step further and incorporate statements of desired program results in authorizing legislation, specifying criteria for measuring these results.

24. *Requiring Program Impact Evaluations.* In the authorizing legislation, Congress should require program impact evaluation of major federal programs.[19] When appropriate, Congress should specify that such studies be based on follow-up samples of program participants and members of relevant comparison groups. Congress should require that these evaluations be done at a level removed from direct control of the program manager–at department level, in the Budget Bureau, or in an office directly responsible to Congress. National program impact evaluations should be required every two to three years.

25. *Providing Resources.* Congress has often assigned responsibility for evaluation of federal programs without allocating staff or financial resources to allow agencies to meet these evaluation responsibilities. Congress should make available to the agencies the funds and staff necessary to carry out the appropriate evaluation studies of major programs.

26. *Congressional Use of Evaluation.* As a part of legislative and appropriations activity, the Congress should ask for and use the results of evaluations. Besides using analytical studies for their

---

19. For an example, see page 80, footnote 28.

own legislative purposes, Congress should also ensure that important policy issues are not being overlooked in Executive Branch
decision making.

THE EXECUTIVE OFFICE[20]

It became clear from this study that the Executive Office of the
President—specifically the Bureau of the Budget (BOB) and the
Council for Urban Affairs—should play a central role in a federal
evaluation system. The Executive Branch had no system for identifying major questions to be answered through evaluation, for
ensuring that high priority studies were carried out, or for ensuring
that significant evaluation findings reached appropriate decision
makers.

Decision making has been closely identified with and geared to
the yearly budget preparations. Rightly so, for this is the means
whereby the President and the Executive Branch spell out their
national priorities—assigning dollars to various goals. The Bureau
of the Budget plays two critical roles in this process:

> The Bureau finds itself trying to get appropriations from Congress for
> Presidential programs and, at times, prodding agencies to come in with
> new or enlarged programs to meet the President's desires (176, p. 35).

The budget time frame—the fiscal year—is a short one, however,
compared to the two or more years required for many program
impact evaluations. Evaluation planning, therefore, must take into
account future policy issues to be addressed by multi-year studies.

The Executive Office can have a major impact on the federal
evaluation process by requiring execution of high priority program
impact evaluations and by reviewing and assessing agency evaluation programs. Because of its present responsibilities and level of
effort, the Bureau of the Budget would be the best place in the
Executive Office to locate this responsibility. When an agency

---

20. Under the reorganization plan proposed by the President on March
12, 1970, and subsequently accepted by the Congress, a new Domestic Council, with a professional staff of 40 to 50, would coordinate policy formula-
tion, and the Bureau of the Budget would be expanded to become a new
Office of Management and Budget, which would place much greater emphasis
on evaluation of program performance than does the present Budget Bureau.

submits its annual program budget estimates, BOB could also require submission of evaluation work plans. These evaluation plans would be reviewed to ensure that evaluation funds were going to answer high priority questions (as determined by the Council for Urban Affairs, the Congress, the federal agencies and the Bureau of the Budget). If agencies were found not to be covering important issues, the Bureau of the Budget should have the capability to undertake its own evaluations.

In addition to reviewing agency evaluation plans, BOB could meet an obvious need: evaluations that cut across agency lines. Only a handful of such studies has been undertaken at the initiative of the agencies themselves (e.g., the current OEO-DOL longitudinal study of five manpower programs). Within the past two years, the Budget Bureau has undertaken two major evaluation studies: an evaluation of the Neighborhood Centers Pilot Program, a precursor of the Model Cities program, for BOB-DOL-HEW-DOD-HUD-OEO (3), and a BOB-VA-DOL-HEW-DOD evaluation of programs for disadvantaged returning veterans. Examples of such direct BOB involvement in evaluation are still rare, however. Neither the examining divisions nor the program evaluation office of BOB has the staff or financial resources to undertake any large number of major evaluation studies, nor has BOB so far shown interest in taking on broad responsibilities for executing evaluations of existing programs.

RECOMMENDATIONS–THE EXECUTIVE OFFICE ROLE

The Nixon administration has placed great emphasis on good management of social programs. In particular, the administration has stressed the need for efficient achievement of lasting results. A major step can be taken toward this end by increasing the role and attention of the Executive Office in evaluation. The following courses of action are recommended:

27. *Presidential Commitment.* The President should continue to emphasize his determination to require and use objective program evaluation in reaching major decisions on the budget and on the administration's legislative program. Only if evaluation studies are clearly seen to affect policy and budget decisions will requests to undertake evaluations carry weight.

28. *Priority Questions.* Through both the Council for Urban Affairs and the Bureau of the Budget, the President should focus attention on major questions to be answered on effectiveness and appropriateness of existing programs. For example: What are the financial and nonfinancial costs and benefits of the various federally funded education programs? What present strategies and techniques are most useful for bringing disadvantaged groups into productive employment? What is the most effective program vehicle for the organizing, planning and delivery of services for an urban area?

29. *Federal Evaluation Plan.* The Bureau of the Budget should be responsible for (a) requiring development of agency evaluation plans, (b) reviewing agency evaluation work plans in the light of decisions required and important questions to be answered over the next two to three years, and (c) using the results of evaluation studies in the budget-making and legislative review processes. Specifically the Bureau of the Budget should:

> Require each federal agency to submit, as part of its budget justification, an annual two- to three-year plan for program impact and program strategy evaluations. Review agency submissions and identify important gaps. Prepare and annually update a two- to three-year government-wide social program evaluation plan that includes both the agency plans and BOB plans for evaluation studies. This plan should be organized by program area.

30. *Inter-Agency Evaluations.* Through the Bureau of the Budget, the President should require initiation of (a) cross-agency evaluations to compare the effectiveness of related federal programs in achieving common objectives and (b) evaluations of techniques used locally to make the best of available federal programs. The Budget Bureau should attempt to accomplish such evaluations through cooperative efforts of the agencies concerned. But if the agencies concerned are unable or unwilling to undertake high priority inter-agency evaluations, the Bureau of the Budget should be given the resources to carry them out.

31. *Requesting Resources.* To implement an evaluation system, the administration should request from Congress evaluation staff and financial resources for the Bureau of the Budget, agency and operating levels. A budget of approximately $3 million per year should be provided for Budget Bureau evaluation of the effectiveness of related programs administered by two or more agencies. At the same time, the President should strongly encourage cabinet

officials to allocate existing staff and money to start or strengthen major evaluation efforts.

FEDERAL AGENCIES

Present assignment of responsibility for the various types of evaluation varies a great deal from agency to agency and from program to program. Whether program-level or agency-level staffs carry out evaluation work may be the result of individual interest, historical accident, or an institutionalized budgeting process. A given program may be the subject of none, one or more of the various kinds of evaluation activity directed by staff at various levels—departmental, agency, subagency, program or operating bureau. Some Office of Education programs, for example, have been the object of evaluation activity at all of these levels: the program branch, the operating bureau, the OE Office of Program Planning and Evaluation, and the HEW Office of Assistant Secretary for Planning and Evaluation.[21]

Evaluation can, of course, be accomplished under a variety of organizational arrangements, depending on where skilled staff can be found to plan and design the required studies and where resources can be located to fund and carry them out.

This study recommends that federal agencies adopt many of the evaluation procedures developed over the past few years at OEO. OEO is singled out as an example because evaluation has been used more effectively in that agency than in the other agencies examined in this study. Consideration of the evaluation structure that evolved there, especially as compared with that of other agencies, enables one to identify critical organizational problems and possible solutions.[22]

---

21. For ease of exposition, the ensuing discussion uses the terms "program-level" and "agency-level" in the following manner. "Program-level" refers to staffs with more responsibility for day-to-day management of a program (e.g., OE's branches and bureaus). "Agency-level" refers to a central staff, detached from program operation, with responsibility for policy decisions across programs (e.g., OE's OPP&E and HEW's ASPE).

22. A supplementary description of the evolution of evaluation at OEO is given in an appendix, printed separately as Urban Institute Working Paper 121-23.

The OEO Model

Prior to 1967, evaluation activity within OEO was left to the discretion of the various program offices.[23] During this period by far the most effort was placed on project monitoring and small-scale studies focusing on program components. Large-scale evaluations based on national samples and using sophisticated research designs with control groups and longitudinal measures of change were almost nonexistent (29). Agency evaluation plans and strategies were lacking.

Several steps were taken early in fiscal year 1968 to rectify this lack and to organize and institutionalize an evaluation system within the agency. They form the basis for the OEO model.

First, evaluation studies were formally classified into three distinct types:

Type I—Program Impact Evaluation: an assessment of overall program impact and effectiveness. The emphasis is on determining the extent to which programs are successful in achieving basic objectives and on the comparative evaluation of national programs.

Type II—Program Strategy Evaluation: an assessment of the relative effectiveness of different program strategies and variables. The emphasis is on determining which program strategies are most productive.

Type III—Project Monitoring: assessment of individual projects through site visits and other activities with the emphasis on managerial and operational efficiency.

Second, there was a reallocation of responsibility for the different types of evaluation. Program impact (Type I) evaluation was placed in the Office of Research, Plans, Programs and Evaluation (RPP&E)[24] at the director's staff level. To handle this task, a new Evaluation Division was established in RPP&E. Responsibility for

---

23. OEO headquarters at the time had three program offices reporting directly to the OEO director: Job Corps, the Community Action Program (CAP), and Volunteers in Service to America (VISTA). The OEO national emphasis programs—Health Services, Upward Bound, Legal Services, Head Start, and Special Field Programs—had separate program offices and evaluation staffs within the CAP structure. Supervision of OEO projects had been delegated to the seven regional offices with headquarters retaining the policy making, planning, and evaluation roles.

24. OEO was reorganized in mid-1969 by the Nixon Administration; RPP&E is now the Office of Planning, Research, and Evaluation.

Types II and III evaluation remained with the individual program offices, which were now required to prepare annual evaluation plans as part of their operating plans. Broadly speaking, responsibilities for the different types of evaluation were placed so as to reflect the operational responsibilities of the offices involved.

Finally, one percent of OEO's total budget was earmarked for evaluation; one-sixth of one percent going to RPP&E for Type I evaluation (approximately $3 million in fiscal year 1969) and five-sixths of one percent remaining in the program offices for Types II and III evaluation.

In combination, these changes were intended to move the evaluation effort off dead center and, in this, OEO was successful. The Evaluation Division moved aggressively to get Type I program impact studies under way. Unlike any other agency, OEO either has planned, is conducting, or has completed studies of the overall impact of all of its major programs. There were some changes in the evaluation practices within individual program offices but few dramatic ones. The Type I evaluation effort consumed most of the Evaluation Division's time, and program offices were left to their own devices. Types II and III evaluation efforts have been somewhat reoriented but remain basically unchanged.

OEO has advanced impressively with evaluation, primarily because of the following: high-level support, strategic location of the central evaluation office, and a well qualified staff devoted solely to this task.

High Level Support

The support of the agency head or program manager is vital for encouraging evaluation. Through formal and informal means, the agency head should ask for, talk about and use evaluations.

All OEO directors have been interested in utilizing analytical studies and procedures. Therefore, evaluation has been taken seriously by the entire agency.[25]

Location of Agency-Level Evaluation

RPP&E was the natural place to locate a central Evaluation Division within OEO because it already had responsibility for budget

25. Compare Marvin and Rouse—Joint Economic Committee. *The Analysis and Evaluation of Public Expenditures: The PPB System* (147).

preparation, analysis related to program planning and basic research. Placing the new Evaluation Division in RPP&E thus gave it access to top political leadership and provided a suitable agency-wide perspective.

Similarly situated offices exist in other agencies. The organization of the Department of Housing and Urban Development, for example, is structurally well adapted for the development of evaluation activities and techniques. Overall leadership responsibility for evaluation is vested in the deputy under secretary for policy analysis and program evaluation, and counterpart planning and evaluation units exist under the several assistant secretaries with program responsibilities. In practice, however, the planning and evaluation units function as small research staffs ministering to the immediate research needs of the deputy under secretary and the assistant secretaries. Formal program evaluation has been a low priority item and has rarely been done.

In addition to the staffs assigned formal responsibility for policy analysis and program evaluation, another HUD group deserves mention in this context. The HUD budget review process is built around the Budget Review Committee. It is chaired by the under secretary and includes as members the assistant secretaries, the general counsel, the deputy under secretary and the federal insurance administrator. Staff service to the committee is provided by HUD's office of budget and the office of the deputy under secretary. The committee's function is to develop for the secretary's consideration a total budget program for the department based on recommendations from assistant secretaries and operating organizations, a comprehensive picture of the alternatives available, and the committee's reasons for proposed choices. Under existing practice, the process stops short of meeting the need for evaluation. The budget review does inquire in depth into the questions, "What services were provided in the past?" and "What is proposed to be done in the future period under consideration?" But it generally has not focused, except tangentially, on the further question, "What have been the effects of the services provided up to now?" Conceptually, this additional element could be built into the existing budget review process, leading to a substantial increase in its usefulness to the management of the department. Such an effort would be facilitated by the fact that the supporting materials prepared for the committee and the order of its consideration are already structured around the PPB program category format developed by the department.

Staff Concentration on Evaluation

OEO's Evaluation Division had a professional staff of five to six to plan and carry out program impact evaluations. The division was not responsible for the demanding budget and planning tasks which RPP&E had to perform. This division of labor has not been the pattern in other agency analytical offices, and consequently their evaluation efforts have suffered.

Since 1966, HEW has had a central analytic staff of approximately 25 staff members, with the assistant secretary for planning and evaluation (ASPE) having responsibility for the planning-programing-budgeting functions. The assistant secretary has the authority for clearance of evaluation plans and individual evaluation studies. At the close of fiscal year 1969, ASPE had enormous department-wide planning and operating responsibilities and a very limited staff. Only one staff member spent the majority of his time on program evaluation.

In HUD, as in HEW, the creative energies of the people capable of the kinds of reflection and analysis required for evaluation have been largely absorbed in meeting other problems. By reason of secretarial, presidential or congressional insistence, available talent was given tasks with characteristically very short lead times, calling for a maximum of ingenuity and improvisation to fit available data into the format of pre-formulated problems. Evaluation has had a low priority under these conditions.

Since the beginning of fiscal 1970, HEW has begun to build an agency-level central evaluation staff within the office of the assistant secretary for planning and evaluation. Similarly, DOL has created a small office of evaluation within the office of the assistant secretary for policy development and research.

Coordinating Role

One problem OEO was not able to handle adequately during 1968 and 1969 was that of coordinating all agency evaluation and evaluation-related activities. That failure to fashion a coordinated system can be attributed to the following factors (which perhaps might be avoided by others):

(1) Although evaluation funds were plentiful, the staff to plan for and administer evaluation funds never was made available to the program offices.

(2) The OEO Evaluation Division was never given the power to coordinate the overall evaluation effort. This would include signing off on each program's annual evaluation plans and on individual evaluation studies. (Had the power existed, the Evaluation Division could not have exercised it effectively with a staff of only six.)

This problem is as bad or worse in other agencies. At the beginning of fiscal 1970, for example, DOL's Manpower Administration found itself in the same position OEO had been in several years earlier. Evaluation was being focused largely on short-term operational monitoring and administrative studies. The whole effort suffered from organizational fragmentation and an unclear delineation of responsibilities for program evaluation of all kinds.

At the time of the study, manpower program evaluation was highly diffused. It took place at the department level under the assistant secretary for policy, evaluation and research (Office of Policy Planning and Research) and under the assistant secretary for administration (Office of Program Review and Audit). The largest part of DOL manpower program evaluation took place in the Manpower Administration, especially in the Office of Evaluation, yet other staff offices also had a piece of the "evaluation pie": the Office of Planning was assigned cost-benefit analysis; the Office of Research independently contracted for a good deal of program strategy evaluation; the Office of Special Manpower Programs evaluated new techniques and program innovations; and the Office of Manpower Management Data Systems independently was assigned the job of creating a data system responsive chiefly to the needs of administrative management. Then, outside the Department of Labor, still further manpower program evaluation was carried out by OEO, HEW and, to some extent, state and local level officials. The Manpower Administration's Office of Evaluation has not had the authority to coordinate these efforts.

Department of Labor personnel are aware of this organizational diffusion of evaluation efforts, as indicated by internal discussion at the Department and program levels. To alleviate the lack of coordination in the Manpower Administration and to provide direction for all DOL manpower evaluation studies, a "Manpower Administration Evaluation Coordinating Committee" has been proposed.

The Office of Economic Opportunity took steps late in 1968 to come to grips with the problem of coordination. OEO's solution was to establish RPP&E's Evaluation Division as a central control point for *all* OEO agency evaluation activities. The following mechanisms were proposed for establishing control and coordination: [26]

(a) Program offices would develop and submit annual evaluation plans to RPP&E. As the central coordinating office, RPP&E would approve all plans.

(b) RPP&E would develop an agency-wide plan based, in part, on program office submissions.

(c) RPP&E would have to approve all RFPs (reviewed for sample size, control groups, etc.).

(d) RPP&E would review reports of actual work against the original RFPs.

Plans also called for reallocating staff slots to strengthen evaluation in the program offices.

Program Level View

Program managers may view evaluation of the impact of their national programs as a process from which they have more to lose than to gain—if not as a threat to their own positions. One possible conclusion of an objective evaluation study, for example, is that the program manager is not performing his job competently, or that the principles underlying a program have proven faulty in whole or in part. In either case, the administrator may prefer to take his chances on ignorance about the worth of the program. There may also be legitimate fears that evaluation might give misinformation or unbalanced views of the worth of programs, either because of the undeveloped state of evaluation methodology or because unsuitable output measures might be chosen by evaluators removed from program responsibilities.

---

26. These proposed changes were overtaken by the OEO reorganization in August 1969.

Within OEO, for example, there has existed a strong difference of opinion on (1) the evaluation classification scheme and (2) the assignment of evaluation responsibilities.

The Resource Management Corporation's study of evaluations of the War on Poverty raised the issue in these terms:

> Although clear-cut distinctions are implied by definitions of Types I, II, and III evaluations, it is difficult to see how in practice their inter-relationships can be minimized. Type II evaluation, for example, is for the purpose of examining the component services of programs. Preferred combinations of components, however, improve the impact that the program will have on the alleviation of poverty. Impact on the alleviation is intended to be the Type I evaluation. However, the Type III evaluation, which is intended to examine the managerial efficiency of programs, also has an effect on Type I evaluations because the efficiency with which a program is managed will also have an effect on the extent to which the ultimate goals are achieved. In sum, the ties between Types I, II, and III evaluations are so strong that separate studies involving each type may be incomplete to the point of yielding misleading results (117, p. 57).

Involved in this dispute were RPP&E's Evaluation Division and, to various degrees, the program offices. RPP&E saw its model as a method of fixing evaluation responsibilities and accomplishing objective national program impact studies. RPP&E viewed the OEO model as a flexible first step taken to get something started. Program offices had a somewhat different perception. They felt threatened by the Type I evaluation, and overpowered by RPP&E. They considered the classification scheme rigid and unrealistic.

Much of the dissatisfaction surfaced at the release by RPP&E of a program impact evaluation of Head Start (174). This study concluded that, "Head Start as it is presently constituted is insufficient as an independent compensatory program in establishing significant cognitive and affective gains which can be supported, reinforced, or maintained in traditional education programs in the primary grade." Program offices considered this report to be narrow, destructive and useless from the standpoint of program improvements. RPP&E defended it as a sound report and a reliable guide to policy planning.[27]

---

27. For a discussion of some of the arguments which resulted see Evans and Williams (29, 1799).

As it stands, the "OEO model" appears to lead to a fragmentation of evaluation efforts in the sense that various types are pictured as being carried out autonomously. Clearly, program impact evaluation can often be carried out in conjunction with program strategy evaluation; program monitoring can be used to classify projects and to determine which projects are operational and therefore worth evaluating. Program strategy evaluation and program monitoring can be useful to those at policy-making levels as well as operating levels. However, RPP&E's efforts to strengthen the program office evaluation staffs and to coordinate all agency evaluation activities have to be viewed as positive moves minimizing the possibility of fragmentation which might result from a too rigid division of evaluation responsibilities. Furthermore, RPP&E's impressive record of initiating program impact evaluations and the negative reaction in program offices to such studies suggest that RPP&E was correct in imposing such a classification and division of responsibilities.

RECOMMENDATIONS–THE FEDERAL AGENCY ROLE

Evaluation is often formally assigned to a "planning and evaluation" unit which has so many program planning and development responsibilities that evaluation is never done or is done very poorly. A series of short-term assignments to each planning and evaluation staff member will prevent the design, execution, and use of (long-term) evaluation studies: "the immediate drives out the ultimate."

32. *Clearly Defined Roles.* Full time staff should be assigned to evaluation to ensure that it receives the continuing attention it deserves at agency and program levels.

33. *Official Support.* Agency heads should (following the example of HEW and OEO) make strong statements about the necessity for program evaluation. They should follow up on these formal statements by building evaluation into agency decision making and by allocating agency-level and operating-level staff and money to evaluation.

34. *Allocation of Responsibility within Agencies.* Evaluation responsibilities should be based on differences in the types of decisions made at policy-making and at operating levels: Policy makers most often are called upon to make choices among

national programs; program managers are most often called upon to make choices of emphasis or decisions on the future of individual projects *within* national programs. To the extent possible, program impact evaluations, designed to discover the worth of an entire national program, should be directed by persons not immediately involved in management of the program and operation. Program strategy evaluation should be directed by persons close enough to the program to introduce variations into the program. Recognizing that circumstances vary from agency to agency and from program to program, we recommend, as at least one way to start getting useful, objective evaluations, that generally departments and agencies should adopt the "OEO model," assigning major evaluation responsibilities roughly as follows:

Evaluation Task	*Level of Responsibility*
Developing evaluation work plans (overall responsibility)	Agency level
Program impact evaluation	Agency level
Program strategy evaluation	Program level
Project rating	Program level
Monitoring	Program level
Disseminating significant results	All levels
Developing methodology	Agency level

(Table 2 translates these generalities into specific recommendations for several of the programs examined during this study. Note that such a division of responsibilities implies that evaluation resources—competent staff and money—will be needed at both agency and program levels.)

35. *Central Evaluation Staff.* Each agency head should establish a central program evaluation staff. This staff should have the resources and authority to accomplish the following tasks:

a. Develop two- to three-year agency-wide or department-wide evaluation work plans.

b. Assist program managers in defining the multiple objectives of their programs and in determining for which of these objectives suitable output measures can be developed.

c. Conduct national program impact evaluations.

d. Assist program managers or their evaluators in designing program strategy evaluations and project rating systems, and in developing improved evaluation methodology.

Table 2. Recommended Assignment of Major Evaluation Responsibilities
for Selected Programs

Assignment	Office of Economic Opportunity (Community Action Program)	Department of Health, Education, and Welfare (Elementary and Secondary Education Programs)	Department of Labor (Manpower Programs)	Department of Housing and Urban Development (Model Cities Programs)
Developing evaluation work plans[a]	OEO Office of Planning, Research, and Evaluation and Community Action Program Office	HEW Assistant Secretary for Planning and Evaluation and OE Deputy Assistant Secretary for Planning, Research, and Evaluation	Assistant Secretary for Policy, Evaluation, and Research and Manpower Administration Office of Evaluation	HUD Deputy Under Secretary and Model Cities Administration Program Development and Evaluation Division
National program impact evaluation[b]	OEO Office of Planning, Research, and Evaluation	HEW Assistant Secretary for Planning and Evaluation and OE Deputy Assistant Secretary for Planning, Research, and Evaluation	Manpower Administration Office of Evaluation and Assistant Secretary for Policy Evaluation, and Research	Model Cities Administration Program Development and Evaluation Division and HUD Deputy Under Secretary[c]
Program strategy evaluation[d]	Community Action Program Office and OEO Office of Planning, Research, and Evaluation	OE Deputy Assistant Secretary for Planning, Research, and Evaluation, and Bureau of Elementary and Secondary Education	Manpower Administration Office of Evaluation	Model Cities Administration Program Development and Evaluation Division
Project rating	Community Action Program Office	OE Bureau of Elementary and Secondary Education	Manpower Administration Office of Evaluation	Model Cities Administration Program Development and Evaluation Division
Monitoring[e]	OEO Regional Offices and Community Action Program Office	Bureau of Elementary and Secondary Education and HEW Regional Offices[f]	DOL Regional Offices and Assistant Secretary for Administration[g]	Model Cities Administration Program Development and Evaluation Division and HUD Regional Offices
Disseminating results of significant evaluation studies	All	All	All	All
Developing evaluation methodology	OEO Office of Planning, Research, and Evaluation and Community Action Program Office	OE Deputy Assistant Secretary for Planning, Research, and Evaluation and HEW Assistant Secretary for Planning and Evaluation	Manpower Administration Office of Evaluation and Assistant Secretary for Policy, Evaluation, and Research	Model Cities Administration Program Development and Evaluation Division and Deputy Under Secretary

[a]Major responsibility for development and review of evaluation work plans should be assigned to the department-level evaluation staff.

[b]Within federal agencies, major responsibility for national program impact evaluation should be assigned to the department-level evaluation staff or to agency (sub-department) evaluation staffs.

[c]The Office of the HUD Deputy Under Secretary has not yet undertaken national program evaluation studies.

[d]Within federal agencies, major responsibility for program strategy evaluation should be assigned to sub-department evaluation staffs and operating-level evaluation staffs working closely with program managers.

[e]All levels will have some interest in monitoring.

[f]The Assistant Secretary for Planning and Evaluation is also establishing a staff for program monitoring.

[g]The Assistant Secretary for Policy, Evaluation, and Research is also taking on some program monitoring responsibilities.

e. Approve the design of all evaluation studies financed by the agency, in particular, ensuring that Requests for Proposals put the planned study in context, specify the objectives and make clear the general strategy to be used.

f. Participate in the planning of field experiments and experimental demonstration projects.

g. Disseminate significant results of evaluation studies to program managers and policy makers, including legislative and budget staffs, and keep records of actions taken on evaluation study recommendations.

h. Assist program-level offices in recruiting and developing evaluation staff.

36. *Evaluation and Research Combination.* Consideration should be given to placing evaluation and research within a single office reporting to the agency head. This action has already been taken in the Office of Economic Opportunity, in the Department of Labor Manpower Administration, and in the Office of Education. This makes it possible to bring together high priority questions, people with the skills to design studies that would answer the questions, and funds for program evaluation studies.

Program Level

Program managers may see evaluation as a disruptive or risky investigation which may fail to grasp the content and objectives of the program or which may be taken out of context. Program managers have much to gain, however, from program strategy evaluation and from project rating—the former to help them identify successful approaches, and the latter to help them identify successful local projects. Therefore, we recommend:

37. *Program Office Responsibilities.* Major responsibility for evaluating projects and alternative strategies *within* programs should rest with the operating bureau chiefs and program managers who know the program and can have some control over input and process variables. On the other hand, operating-level plans for experiments and evaluations should be reviewed and approved at agency level to determine whether they give adequate attention to gathering the kinds of data needed for higher-level decisions.

38. *Evaluation Divisions.* Major operating bureaus (and, in some cases, individual programs) should establish evaluation divisions

reporting to the bureau chief, with responsibility for (1) developing two- to three-year evaluation work plans, (2) helping program managers define program objectives in measurable terms, (3) conducting program strategy and project rating evaluations, and (4) disseminating the results of significant evaluation studies to program managers and policy makers at relevant federal, state, and local levels.

39. *Experimentation.* Managers of operating programs should be given responsibility for introducing planned variations and possibly even controlled experiments into a small portion of their operating program or into a related experimental demonstration program.

STATE AND LOCAL LEVELS

The evaluation of federal social programs is complicated by the fact that most are administered by state and local governments or other public agencies. A great many federal programs are already administered through the states, and the Administration has proposed decentralizing other programs (for example, the manpower programs) to the states. In such cases, federal funds often lose their identity and become simply a part of state grants to localities. Yet federal responsibilities in most of these programs go beyond financing of services to improving the capability of state and local levels to manage their funds and reach their objectives.

A long tradition of local autonomy and the lack of precedents for federal monitoring of local efforts (e.g., in state grant-in-aid programs and in education programs) often leads to reluctance on the part of federal managers to insist on evaluation of such programs, even when the federal input is substantial. Administrators in the Office of Education Division of Vocational Education, for example, argue that since their programs are implemented at the local level, they should be evaluated there—even though, they admit, local resources for evaluation are minimal. Owing partly to this reluctance, the division has no formal system for evaluating vocational education programs.

What should the federal government do in such program areas? Where federal funds pay part or all of the cost of state- or locally-

oriented programs, it is appropriate that federal evaluation strategy for such programs has two main thrusts:

> Sponsorship of field experiments and experimental demonstration proj-
> ects to systematically test promising program strategies and compo-
> nents. Results of the evaluations would be disseminated to state and
> local levels.
>
> Financial support and technical assistance to groups of cooperating
> states and localities that face similar problems and that agree to work
> together. They should use common methodology to evaluate the rela-
> tive effectiveness of alternative approaches to solving their problems.

In a number of program areas, as under Title I of the Elementary and Secondary Education Act, a good deal of money and
effort is being expended on local project evaluations conducted
simply to meet formal evaluation requirements. Lack of comparability of these studies makes it impossible to learn much from
them at the state or national level. The undeveloped state of
methodology for evaluating individual local projects makes it difficult or impossible to assess the significance of most of these "evaluations." To cite only one problem, control groups developed
through random assignment to treatment and non-treatment categories usually are not available. Allowing localities complete
freedom in designing and conducting their own evaluations results
in large numbers of small, unrelated studies that offer policy
makers and program managers cloudy insights at great cost to the
federal government.

To counteract such wasteful practices, federal agencies should
consider the following approaches:

> *Programs administered by states.* Cooperative arrangements among the
> states should be encouraged to test common approaches to evaluation
> of similar state programs. Then an evaluation of compensatory educa-
> tion programs, for instance, conducted in California could supplement
> the results of a study conducted in New York, and vice versa. To foster
> such cooperation, the federal government should consider making
> grants for evaluation to *groups* of states, on the condition that they
> cooperate in searching for effective program strategies and techniques.
> For example, the Office of Education in cooperation with 27 states is
> developing a coordinated approach to collection and analysis of data on
> all federally-supported elementary and secondary education programs.

Programs administered by local governments. Through federal evaluation guidelines, financial support and technical assistance, local communities should be encouraged to cooperate in federal and state efforts to collect and analyze comparable data.

Groups of cities. Groups of large and medium-sized cities and groups of small communities should be encouraged to develop their own systems for evaluation of local programs through collection and analysis of comparable data. This should be encouraged by federal funds and technical assistance. Several cities working together could, for example, set up an experimental design to test alternative program strategies in schools serving similar student populations and thus make crucial comparisons.

A number of local school systems and community groups are now beginning to define objectives for their school programs and to make schools more accountable to the public. Such a process coupled with comparable local evaluations could do a good deal to upgrade the quality of education in this country, especially if the Office of Education developed useful prototype systems for assessing educational outcomes for comparable groups of children.

RECOMMENDATIONS–STATE AND LOCAL CONSIDERATIONS

40. *Federal Surveillance.* Whenever federal funds are being expended to support state and local activities, the federal government should retain some evaluation role to discharge its duty to administer public funds efficiently. Agencies should help determine what types of evaluation are appropriate.

41. *Comparability.* Federal funds generally should not be expended on unrelated, noncomparable evaluations of individual local projects.

42. *Cooperative Efforts.* In a large number of program areas, federal, state and local governments should work together to establish cooperative mechanisms for objective evaluation of alternative program strategies under varying circumstances. Cooperative efforts should provide for systematic examination of major program variations; collection of comparable data on costs, processes and outputs; and collection of comparable follow-up data to show the impact of different approaches. For example, if administration of the manpower programs is delegated to the states, the federal government should support cooperative arrangements among

states to evaluate alternative manpower program approaches on similar target groups.

43. *Evaluation Priorities.* For programs like education, in which state and local governments contribute the major share of funds with support from federal grants, federal agencies should rely largely on program strategy evaluation, in conjunction with field experiments or experimental demonstration programs, and on development and demonstration of project rating systems for use at state and local levels.

5. Evaluation Resources

Only in the last few years have federal agency staffs been given any substantial resources for social program evaluation. Based on examination of fifteen programs in four federal agencies, this chapter presents estimates of the financial and in-house staff resources needed for accomplishing sound, useful evaluations of federal programs. Funding and staffing are related, because the effective use of evaluation funds depends on recruiting and retaining in-house skilled evaluation staff members.

FUNDS

Unless legislation or agency policy specifically earmarks funds, evaluation staffs will not be assembled nor the evaluation job done. Only when a flow of resources exists will a formal responsibility to evaluate be translated into significant evaluation activities. This is evident from the record of evaluation in the four agencies examined in this study:

> In the Department of Housing and Urban Development, only very limited funds have been available for evaluation studies. Hence little HUD program evaluation was done on a systematic and continuing basis before the recent availability of substantial funds for evaluation of the Model Cities program.

> In the Department of Labor, evaluation of manpower programs has been dramatically upgraded as a result of the availability of adequate funds under the Economic Opportunity Act and under the Social Security Amendments of 1967.

77

In the Department of Health, Education and Welfare, the most highly developed research and evaluation system is found in the Social Security Administration because it can tap trust funds to support such efforts. On the other hand, evaluations of Medicaid and the Title I elementary and secondary education program have suffered because of inadequate financing.

The Office of Economic Opportunity was able to develop an extensive evaluation system because of the commitment of substantial resources: one-sixth of one percent of OEO appropriations for agency-level evaluation by the Office of Planning, Research, and Evaluation, and at least five-sixths of one percent of OEO appropriations for evaluation by program managers.

Table 3 shows how evaluation funding varies widely in the agencies and programs examined. Noteworthy are the following details about the amounts and percentages of program funds used.

Evaluation has been grossly underfunded in the Office of Education. Only $1.25 million per year has been specifically authorized for program evaluation and only $3 to $4 million per year—one-tenth of one percent—of OE appropriations have been spent on evaluation at the Federal level. OE, with a budget of $3.5 billion, has had not much more money to evaluate all its programs than OEO had to evaluate its $330 million Head Start program alone. (HEW Secretary Finch requested authority to allocate up to one percent of education funds to evaluation. Congress did not accept this formula but did vote more than $9 million for this purpose for fiscal year 1970.)

Evaluation of Manpower Development and Training programs has been grossly underfunded. Research and administrative funds for evaluation amounted to only 0.1 percent of program appropriations in fiscal year 1969. Almost all of the funds the Manpower Administration did get in 1969 for evaluation funds, in fact, were made available through delegated monies from OEO and HEW. In fiscal year 1969, the central analytic staffs in three Departments—Health, Education and Welfare, Housing and Urban Development, and Labor—directly controlled *no* evaluation funds, whereas the OEO Office of Planning, Research, and Evaluation had available more than $2.5 million for evaluation studies.

The Economic Opportunity Act is broad enough to authorize and require expenditure of program funds for evaluation. OEO has found that 1 percent of program funds was approximately the right percentage for

Table 3. 1969 Funding and In-House Staff for Evaluation of Selected Programs[a]

Department	(1) Estimated 1969 Obligations (Millions)	(2) Estimated 1969 Federal Evaluation Contracts and Grants (Millions)[b]	(3) Percentage for Evaluation[b] [(2)/(1)]	(4) Estimated In-House Professional Evaluation Staff
Total (selected programs)	*3,877*	*17.0*	*0.4*	*76*
Department of Labor (selected programs)	*1,010*	*4.1*	*0.4*	*28*
Manpower Development and Training Programs[c]	240	0.3	0.1	
Programs funded under the Economic Opportunity Act[d]	665	2.8[l]	0.4	28
Work Incentive Program[e]	105	1.0	1.0	
Department of Health, Education, and Welfare (selected programs)	*1,610*	*4.0*	*0.3*	*26*
Maternal and Child Health Programs[f]	210	1.4	0.7	13
Vocational Education[g]	250	0.1[m]	0.03	1+
Title I, Elementary and Secondary Education Act	1,120	0.6	0.05	9
Follow Through[h]	30	1.9	6.3	3
Office of Economic Opportunity (selected programs)	*1,003*	*6.5*	*0.7*	*14*
Community Action Program (local initiative programs only)[i]	331	2.2[n]	0.7	7
Head Start[j]	330	2.4	0.7	2
Job Corps[k]	295	1.9[o]	0.6	4
Legal Services Program	47	0[p]	0	1
Department of Housing and Urban Development (selected programs)	*254*	*2.4*	*0.9*	*8*
Model Cities	254	2.4	0.9	8

[a]Because of delays in fiscal year 1970 appropriations and because of the lack of agency evaluation plans, 1970 funding estimates and evaluation funding estimates are still not available for most programs.

[b]Including contracts for development of evaluation systems but *excluding* costs for in-house staff, administrative costs for monitoring activities, and some costs for data collection. Because of the use of multiple funding sources for evaluation and because of the lack of overall agency evaluation plans, these figures must be considered "best estimates" only.

[c]Institutional programs (delegated to HEW) and on-the-job training programs.

[d]Neighborhood Youth Corps, Operation Mainstream, New Careers, Concentrated Employment Program, Special Impact Program; includes JOBS program but excludes Job Corps.

[e]Delegated from HEW.

[f]Grant-in-aid programs for maternal and child health services and crippled children's services, project grants for maternity and infant care, family planning, and comprehensive health care for children, and appropriations for research and training.

[g]Vocational Education Act of 1963 and George Barden Act only.

[h]Funded from the Head Start program appropriation.

[i]Does not include national emphasis programs, such as Head Start and the Legal Services Program.

[j]Now transferred to HEW.

[k]Now transferred to Department of Labor.

[l]Includes $750,000 OEO share of the Comparative Manpower Program Evaluation Study on the Job Corps, MDTA (Institutional), NYC (Out-of-School), JOBS, and New Careers programs.

[m]Approximately $350,000 was obligated during fiscal year 1968 for Vocational Education evaluation.

[n]Includes costs for program impact and program strategy evaluations of CAP, including local initiative programs but excluding national emphasis programs such as Head Start and the Legal Services Program.

[o]Excludes OEO share of cost of the Comparative Manpower Program Evaluation Study. (See footnote [l] above.)

[p]Legal Services Program expended approximately $300,000 for monitoring contracts.

evaluation in fiscal years 1968 and 1969. In 1967 and 1968, Congress enacted amendments providing for funding of HEW evaluation under 11 pieces of legislation.[28]

The Department of Housing and Urban Development allocated more than $2 million to Model Cities program evaluation in 1969 and is requiring city demonstration agencies to allocate 3 to 5 percent of Model Cities supplementary grants to data collection and evaluation.

The Follow Through elementary education program, a small experimental demonstration program designed to test the worth of a number of strategies for educating disadvantaged children, spent about 6 percent of its 1969 budget on evaluation.

All programs do not require the same level of funds for evaluation. The appropriate level—best expressed as a percentage of a program's annual budget—varies according to the following considerations:

Type and stage of development of program. Field experiments and experimental demonstration programs, for example, will require greater funds for evaluation than certain well-established programs that have proven their worth and thus may require limited evaluation, if any, at a particular point in time.

Size of program. On a percentage basis, small programs tend to cost more to evaluate than larger programs.

---

28. Up to 1 percent of program appropriations may be reserved by the Secretary of Health, Education and Welfare for evaluation of the programs authorized under the following laws: *Public Health Service Act*—1.) Sec. 309(c)(2), grants to schools of public health; 2.) Sec. 314(d)(1), formula grants for public health services; 3.) Sec. 314(e), project grants for public health services; 4.) Sec. 797, allied health professions; and 5.) Sec. 901(a), regional medical programs; *Community Mental Health Centers Act*, Sec. 262 (Sec. 303(a) of P.L. 90-574); *Juvenile Delinquency Prevention and Control Act*, Sec. 404 of P.L. 90-445; *Vocational Rehabilitation Act*, Sec. 7(e) (up to $1 million).

Up to ½ of 1 percent of program appropriations may be reserved by the Secretary for evaluation under the Social Security Act, Sec. 513(b), maternal and child health.

Such sums as may be necessary may be appropriated by Congress for evaluation under the following two laws: Education programs, Public Law 90-247—blanket authorization in Sec. 402; Work Incentive Program, Sec. 441 of the Social Security Act.

Types of decisions required. Decisions about alternative approaches, for example, may require costly program strategy evaluations whereas program impact information usually can be obtained at lower cost.

Probability that findings will be used. The greater the likelihood that program decisions will be influenced by evaluation, the greater the justification for raising the spending level.

Availability of methodology. Funds should be concentrated on evaluations where it is feasible to get meaningful answers—manpower training programs, for example—but withheld or used sparingly where methodology is poor—as in urban renewal or community action programs.

Program strategy evaluation and project rating could be financed through expenditure of program funds in those cases where program funds may be spent for technical assistance to states and localities. Such possibilities appear to exist, for example, for the DOL Manpower Development and Training program and HUD's Model Cities program. In the latter case, Section 106 of the Demonstration Cities and Metropolitan Development Act states, "The Secretary is authorized to undertake such activities as he determines to be desirable to provide . . . *technical assistance* to city demonstration agencies to assist such agencies in planning, developing, and administering comprehensive city demonstration programs" (emphasis added). Evaluation studies financed under this provision—for which HUD planned to spend up to $9 million in 1970—have to be directly related, of course, to the needs of local city demonstration agencies.

RECOMMENDATIONS—FUNDING

44. *Budgeting.* Each agency head should know for each major social program what funds are available for evaluation. These funds may be labeled as "evaluation" monies, but they also may be included in appropriations for research, technical assistance, training, program operation and program administration. Next, agency heads should know how the funds are allocated among programs and among the major types of evaluation. On the basis of these facts, and in light of considerations mentioned in other chapters, a reasonable level of funding for evaluation can be determined. If necessary, the Administration should have legislation introduced to allow the agency head to set aside the necessary amount for evaluation.

45. *Funding Levels.* A reasonable evaluation budget, this study suggests, is likely to range from 0.5 percent to 2 percent of the total program budget. For the programs in Table 3 which do not yet have legislation allowing the agency head to earmark a portion of program funds for evaluation, for example, it would appear reasonable, based on factors discussed elsewhere, to allocate up to 2 percent of manpower program funds, up to 0.5 percent of vocational education funds, and up to 0.5 percent of Title I elementary and secondary education funds to program evaluation.

46. *Nonlegislated Money Sources.* In the absence of legislation allowing the use of a portion of program funds for evaluation, agencies should draw funds for evaluation from their budgets for research and general administration. In certain cases, budgets for technical assistance to states and localities can be used to finance program strategy evaluations and project ratings.

47. *United Effort.* The agencies should be supported by the President, the Budget Bureau and the Congress in requests for adequate funding of evaluation work.

STAFFING

A major obstacle to evaluation has been the lack of highly qualified agency-level and operating program-level staffs devoting full time to evaluation. Such personnel are essential for help in defining program objectives and output measures, developing evaluation work plans, designing studies and methodologies, carrying out studies, reviewing proposals and monitoring the work of contractors, and disseminating findings and recommendations.

In many agencies and programs, evaluation is a part-time assignment tacked on to the duties of staff members who have other full-time responsibilities. Owing to the press of these other obligations, evaluation tends to come last—if it comes at all. The Social Security Administration's Office of Research and Statistics and the OEO Office of Planning, Research, and Evaluation, each with a substantial in-house evaluation capability, are notable bright spots in an otherwise bleak staff picture. When this study began, the Office of Economic Opportunity had a full-time, agency-level evaluation staff.[29] The Departments of Labor,

_____

29. The OEO Evaluation Division was fully occupied in design and execution of national program impact evaluation studies and did not put much

Housing and Urban Development, and Health, Education and Welfare did not. Since July 1, 1969, both Labor and HEW have created agency-level evaluation staffs.

At operating program level, where program strategy evaluation and project rating are among the most challenging tasks to be done, program managers are typically handicapped by insufficient positions and low grade-levels. Even when positions are available, managers have difficulty in attracting skilled researchers. The Office of Education Bureau of Elementary and Secondary Education, for example, has had a recruiting problem ever since it was established. OEO program officers said they were not handicapped by lack of evaluation funds but by a critical shortage of in-house staff to use those funds efficiently. Part of the recruiting problem results from the poor image that university professors and students have of federal program evaluation. Program strategy evaluation positions could become very desirable research positions, however, particularly if evaluators are given responsibility for introducing structural variations into portions of operating programs or for designing field experiments or experimental demonstration programs.

For the foreseeable future, staff limitations will force most agencies and program managers to rely heavily on contractors to carry out evaluation studies. The effective use of evaluation contractors, however, itself demands the presence of highly skilled in-house staffs, not only when an evaluation contract is first being considered but also while the work progresses and when it is completed.

Examples of inadequate in-house evaluation staffs are too numerous to list. A dramatic example of understaffing was in Head Start where only three or four professional staff members were given responsibility for an annual research and evaluation budget of $6 million. (Changes have taken place in the planning and management of Head Start, but the size of its research and evaluation staff is still inadequate.)

Table 3 presents estimates of the number of staff devoted to evaluation of selected federal programs. In relation to evaluation funds available, the Head Start program had the most severe

emphasis on development of agency-wide evaluation work plans or assistance to operating-level program managers or evaluation staffs.

staffing problems. One to two Head Start staff members have been responsible for monitoring approximately $2.5 million a year in evaluation contracts and grants. They have been unable to give adequate direction to this level of effort.

The OEO Evaluation Division, on the other hand, has five professionals to manage contracts amounting to approximately $3 million. An Evaluation Division staff member is usually responsible for one or two major studies. He develops the work statement and Request for Proposals for a study, helps choose an evaluation contractor, works closely with the contractor, and presents significant findings and recommendations arising from the study.

As a rule of thumb, agency-level and operating program-level evaluation staffs will require one in-house evaluation staff member at the level of GS-13 to GS-15 or higher for every two to four studies—or $500,000 worth of studies—under contract or grant. Additional staff members are required for carrying out other specific functions—developing work plans, shaping field experiments and experimental demonstrations, defining objectives, devising output measures and reporting requirements, and making findings known to policy makers.

RECOMMENDATIONS–STAFFING

48. *Full-Time Staffs.* Full-time evaluation staffs should be created at department/agency and operating bureau/program levels.

49. *Numbers.* Evaluation staffs should include at least one professional staff member for every two to four ongoing studies (or $500,000 worth of ongoing studies) to be done under contracts or grants, in addition to staff members required to develop evaluation work plans, help define program objectives and output measures, help define program reporting requirements, help shape plans for field experiments and experimental demonstration programs, and ensure that significant results of evaluation studies are brought to the attention of program managers and policy makers.

50. *Effective Use of Time.* Since each study annually may require the use of a half man-year of in-house staff time to design an evaluation, to review study proposals, to monitor the execution of the study, and to ensure that significant findings and recommendations reach appropriate policy makers and program managers, agencies with small evaluation staffs but adequate evaluation funds

should concentrate these funds on small numbers of relatively large studies.

51. *Qualifications.* Most evaluation staffs should include both people with agency or program background and people with advanced training in such fields as economics, statistics, mathematics, systems analysis and experimental design. Interns with recent training in quantitative analysis may be another source of needed skills. Existing planning and research staff members are likely candidates for evaluation staff positions.

52. *Operating-Level Needs.* Since some of the most challenging evaluation tasks (program strategy evaluation, project rating, and design of experiments and experimental demonstration programs) will most appropriately be accomplished at bureau/operating program level, the tendency to reserve high grade-level evaluation positions for department/agency level staffs should be resisted.

53. *Recruiting.* The central evaluation staff in each agency should be given responsibility for helping to recruit and train staff members for evaluation positions throughout the agency.

54. *Contract Assistance.* Agencies faced with strict constraints on a number of in-house evaluation staff positions should consider use of contractors to assist in preparation of evaluation work plans and in design of evaluation studies (including preparation of work statements for inclusion in subsequent Requests for Proposals), recognizing that significant inputs of in-house staff time will still be required. Conversely, because of the amount of in-house staff time required to set up contracted studies, agencies should when possible consider placing more emphasis on doing parts of evaluation studies in-house, in such cases using contractors only for clearly specified subtasks.

6. Methodology

Essential conditions for successful evaluation of a federal program are the existence of the methodology and sound measurements that will make it possible to distinguish the program's effects, if any, from the effects of all the other forces working in a situation—to isolate what happened as a result of the program from what would probably have happened anyway. As might be expected, these conditions are not always met. Consider the situation where the federal financial input is dwarfed by local inputs, as in the Title I elementary and secondary education program. Unless the proportion of federal funds varies widely from project to project or the program is being operated as a tightly controlled experiment, it will not be possible to isolate the effect of the federal dollars.

Other factors that can interfere with successful evaluation of federal programs include variations of the social context in which the program operates. A training program designed to give high school dropouts a technical skill may be inherently sound, reflecting a thoughtful process of instruction and a careful analysis of employment demands. Regardless of the intrinsic quality of the program, however, its intended result—enabling teenagers to secure jobs with a future—may fall short of expectations for several reasons such as the following which have nothing to do with the merits of the program itself:

The loss or reduction of major contracts may force industry in a particular area to cut back its work force, the most recently hired workers

86

being fired first as has happened in the automotive industry. An unexpected technological development may reduce the need for a particular skill which earlier appeared to be in a "growth" area—as has happened in the case of key-punch operation.

A major social trend may affect employment—as growing public sentiment against smoking would affect not only employment in the tobacco industry, but also in the advertising and television industries.

This chapter explores the methodological tasks to be accomplished in carrying out evaluations, draws tentative conclusions on the methodological feasibility of the various types of evaluation for the programs examined, and recommends priorities among possible evaluation studies, field experiments and experimental demonstration projects.

POTENTIAL OF RESEARCH DESIGN AND METHOD

Social programs are evaluated to ascertain whether elements built into them are really accomplishing what was intended. Without clear measures of program accomplishment—unconfounded with the effects of other programs and of the environment—there exists no sure basis for making a decision about the relative value of the program or any element of it.

The principles of modern experimental design provide the basis for estimating the amounts and directions of program effects. Experimental design allows us to test hypotheses about program effects in such a way that the effects of extraneous factors can be excluded or corrected for, clearing the way for reasonable inferences about those factors in which we are interested. If the extraneous factors are no longer a threat to adequate inference, we are then in a position to rule out—among the set of "plausible" hypotheses—those which are not sustained by the results given by the study.

Following Campbell and Stanley, and Suchman, Table 4 presents a classification of evaluation research designs (14, 142). Here X represents the exposure of a group to a social action program, the effects of which are to be measured. An O refers to the process of measuring effects. The X's and O's in the same row refer to the same persons—either receiving treatment (X) or being measured (O). Temporal order is left-to-right. The symbol R indicates ran-

Table 4. Variations in Evaluation Research Designs[a]

Pre-Experimental Designs:

1. One-Shot Case Study   X   0
   (weakest but most common evaluation
   research design)

2. One-Group, Pre-Test/Post-Test Design....................................... O_1 X O_2
   (does not permit one to attribute
   changes to the program being evaluated)

3. The Static Group Comparison ....   X O_1
   (affords no way of knowing that the two O_2
   groups were equivalent *before* the program)

True Experimental Designs (particularly applicable to field experiments and to experimental demonstration projects):

4. Pre-Test/Post-Test, Control Group Design ....
   R O_1 X O_2
   R O_3 O_4

5. Solomon Four–Group Design ....
   R O_1 X O_2
   R O_3 O_4
   (controls and measures both the experimental
   R   X O_5
   effect and the possible interaction effects of
   R O_6
   the measuring process itself)

6. Post-Test Only, Control Group Design ....
   R   X O_1
   R O_2

7. Comparison of Alternative Program Strategies ....
   R O_1 X_1 O_2
   R O_3 X_2 O_4
   R O_5 X_3 O_6
   R O_7 O_8

Quasi-Experimental Designs:

8. Nonequivalent Comparison Group Design ....
   O_1 X O_2
   O_3 O_4
   (well worth using in many instances in
   which Designs 4, 5, and 6 are impossible)

9. Comparison of Alternative Program Strategies,
   Comparison of Local Projects ....
   O_1 X_1 O_2
   O_3 X_2 O_4
   O_5 X_3 O_6
   O_7 O_8

10. Time-Series Design ....
    O_1 O_2 O_3 O_4 X O_5 O_6 O_7 O_8

11. Multiple Time-Series Design ....
    O_1 O_2 O_3 O_4 X O_5 O_6 O_7 O_8
    (excellent quasi-experimental design,
    O_9 O_{10} O_{11} O_{12} O_{13} O_{14} O_{15} O_{16}
    perhaps the best of the more feasible
    designs)

[a] Adapted from Campbell and Stanley (14) and Suchman (142). Campbell and Stanley present a much more extensive list of quasi-experimental designs.

dom assignment to separate treatment groups; rows not preceded by the symbol R indicate comparison groups not equated by random assignment.

The "strength" of a design is the degree to which it eliminates threats to valid inference. The "strongest" are the "true" experimental designs, numbers 4, 5, 6 and 7. They include the critical basis for valid inference in most situations—random allocation of participants to treatment and to control groups—thus automatically ruling out extraneous-source "explanations" of the effects of a given treatment. The "weakest" are the non-experimental designs, numbers 1, 2 and 3. They are vulnerable to such problems as seasonal trends or random variability in the external environment, maturation, and attrition in the treatment group over time.[30] Quasi-experimental designs are stronger but, without the benefit of random assignment, one cannot be certain that the experimental and comparison groups are equivalent.

Designs 1, 2, 3, 4, 5, 6, 8, 10 and 11 are possible designs for program impact evaluations, local project evaluations, or field experiments. Numbers 7 and 9 are possible designs for program strategy evaluation or for project rating. The choice of design depends on such conditions as cost, ability to implement, level of confidence required—all related to methodological factors. Suchman summarized the three main conditions of the experimental method as they apply to evaluative research:

1. Sampling equivalent experimental and control groups (or performing statistical analyses to approximate the controlled conditions of the laboratory experiment).

2. Definition and measurement of criteria of effect.

3. Isolation and control of the stimulus (treatment).

The following sections examine the implications of each of these conditions for federal evaluation efforts.

SAMPLING EQUIVALENT "EXPERIMENTAL" AND "CONTROL" GROUPS

A prime requirement for evaluation is the sampling of equivalent experimental (treatment) and control (non-treatment) groups. In a controlled experiment, equivalence is obtained by random assignment of individuals to treatment and non-treatment. There is al-

---

30. Campbell and Stanley list 12 threats—or extraneous hypotheses—to valid inference (14).

most universal agreement among evaluators and program managers, however, on the difficulty or impossibility of random assignment of individuals for evaluation of operating programs or of local projects within programs. Even very costly, sophisticated evaluation efforts (such as the million-dollar-per-year Educational Testing Service longitudinal Head Start evaluation) almost always rely instead on statistical techniques, such as covariance analysis, that attempt to approximate the comparisons that would be made in true experiments.

The practical considerations involved are typified in the development of guidelines for evaluation of Title I ESEA programs, late in 1965. The initial guidelines were prepared under contract by professors of education at Colorado State and Pennsylvania State Universities. Because of the tradition of local control of education, there was an implicit decision by the Office of Education to set evaluation standards that were *not* made uniform for local school systems. The notion of control groups was rejected at the outset because this implied that "some deserving Title I kids must be denied services for the sake of experimentation." The states immediately rejected control groups, claiming that Title I was not a research program. The Title I evaluation guidelines were 10 pages of alternative theories of educational evaluation. Local districts were expected to choose the theory that best fit local conditions; national standards were not set.

A similar situation was described by one evaluator of the Head Start program.

> From the standpoint of pure research, it is regrettable that virtually none of the Head Start research has been truly experimental—that is, based upon comparison of the subsequent developments of treatment and control groups randomly drawn from the same population of eligible children and randomly assigned to Head Start or non-Head Start status. While it must be conceded that such procedure would be patently outrageous with respect to the purposes and policies of Head Start . . . that limitation introduces unknowable biases into the research designs which have been employed; interpretations of such evidence are necessarily matters of judgment, rather than matters of fact (174).

From the point of view of the evaluator, there are several things wrong with this attitude that it "would be patently outrageous" to use control groups when they are needed. First, the resources to be devoted to social programs are often quite limited. Thus, not everyone who might be eligible for benefits can be accepted in the program. So some selection device already is used, meaning that some people are screened in and some are screened out. Use of a randomly selected control group simply introduces a set of "non-treatment" subjects in a roughly uniform fashion throughout the whole group of treatment subjects. This implies the need to modify the cutoff points of the selection procedure in order to satisfy a random selection requirement. Since selection procedures in social programs tend to be fuzzy at the margins anyway—and often along much of the whole worthy-of-selection line—the use of control groups selected on a random allocation basis would not seem to be seriously subject to the denial-of-benefit charge.

A second argument for control group usage centers around the basic question that the evaluation is examining—whether the treatment does, in fact, convey any benefits. The experience of social program evaluations in the past few years would seem to indicate that, *a priori*, one cannot expect much in the way of highly valued benefits as the result of a social program. Therefore, the expected value of the information increment from using control groups could presumably be higher than the expected value of the loss of benefits. Until social programs begin to show much greater payoffs much more often, a policy of using control groups would seem to be a very good investment. Furthermore, if the value of the program is high, then it will be more readily accepted over the long run if testing brings objective evidence of the program's benefits. In this sense, those treatments which are effective would be applied to far more people in the long run, in exchange for foregoing treatment to a control group in the short run. This is similar to the argument used in clinical trials, where drugs are withheld from patients as part of an experimental design—with the public at large benefiting from caution about what is financed and offered until efficacy is proven.

In spite of its value, one must admit the operational difficulties facing any evaluation that attempts to specify random assignment. If such sophistication is seen as critical, then it may be more feasible to turn from evaluation of on-going programs to experiments or experimental demonstration projects, where the evaluator can have more administrative control over inputs and process.

In practice, control groups usually have not been used, and reliance has been placed on the use of "matched" comparison groups and statistical techniques. There can be real problems, however, in finding appropriate comparison groups. Two Job Corps evaluations, one using "no shows" as a comparison group and the other using later Job Corps enrollees as a comparison group, reached widely different conclusions on the value of Job Corps: the first study estimated benefit-cost ratios between 0.97 and 1.70, the second study estimated benefit-cost ratios of 4.5 to 5.0. This led one observer to note: "This is a disturbing situation. Evaluation findings relating to the same reality may vary from submarginal to excellent, depending on the assumptions and attitudes of the analyst (118, p. 193)."

Aside from the problems of getting equivalent comparisons there is the added difficulty of administering a large study with comparison groups. Stanford Research Institute's 1968-1969 Follow Through evaluation used a sample of 2,598 pupils from 137 program classrooms and 1,461 pupils from 64 non-program comparison classrooms. Follow Through has had continuing problems in developing appropriate comparison groups, either in Follow Through communities or in non-Follow Through communities. It is extremely difficult to talk non-Follow Through principals into participating in or cooperating in the evaluation, since they see nothing to gain. In addition, SRI staff members who have been visiting Follow Through classrooms and non-Follow Through classrooms have noticed that Follow Through ideas are being picked up in other classrooms in the same community. Possibility of this sort of diffusion would make it unwise to use non-Follow Through children in the same community as controls for Follow Through children: if both experimental and comparison groups make progress, the evaluation might give too pessimistic a view of the results achieved.

The Follow Through staff has not felt politically strong enough to make random assignments of Follow Through program models to communities. The Follow Through research design does not, therefore, furnish any protection against the possibility (and the fact) of self-selection as an uncontrolled input variable. Subsequent differences achieved by the program models may reflect initial differences in communities rather than in program content. It has been suggested that Follow Through-like programs could get past the political difficulty of random assignment of treatments to communities by offering each community a limited range of choices of program models.[31]

RECOMMENDATIONS–COMPARISON GROUPS

55. *Common Objectives.* The difficulty of denying treatment to individuals for purposes of "research" (evaluation) and practical difficulties in collecting data on "control" individuals argue strongly for evaluation studies that attempt to determine the relative effectiveness of two or more program strategies or two or more national programs in achieving common objectives.

56. *Demonstration Projects.* Experimental demonstration projects in a particular program should be set up with a common evaluation design allowing for comparison of results—using the participants in different projects as comparison groups for one another.

57. *Overall Study Design.* Federal money generally should not be spent on evaluation of individual local projects unless they have been developed as field experiments, with equivalent treatment and control groups.

58. *High-Level Review.* In each demonstration or pilot program, Congress and the Budget Bureau should require a statement of the experimental demonstrations to be carried out and a description of the system to be used for comparing different strategies and techniques.

DEFINING EFFECTIVENESS CRITERIA AND MEASURING EFFECTS

A social program operates under a hierarchy of objectives—short term, intermediate, and long term. The different levels are related by a chain of assumptions that certain program activities (aimed at short term or sub-objectives) result in the attainment of certain effects (intermediate and long-term goals). For example, putting a low-skilled unemployed male through a training and job placement program assumes at least that his motivation and future employability will increase and, in the end, his employment and income will be improved.

---

31. Private communication from David Cohen, Harvard Graduate School of Education.

In practice, the problem of evaluation criteria has been one of a lack of specificity in program objectives (particularly when the authorizing legislation was very general) and lack of emphasis on ultimate objectives expressed in terms of types of outputs to be achieved through the program. Proper definitions of objectives for manpower training programs, for example, would presumably stress increased earnings and reduced unemployment for particular population groups rather than number of job placements. Even when ultimate program objectives are defined, there often remain problems of defining suitable intermediate objectives and suitable long-term and short-term output measures.

Suchman (142) has proposed five categories of criteria according to which the success or failure of a program may be evaluated:

1. *Effort.* The criterion of success is the quantity and quality of activity that takes place; it is an assessment of input (workload) without regard to output.

2. *Effectiveness.* This is a performance criterion measuring the results of effort rather than the effort itself; it requires a clear statement of objectives.

3. *Impact.* The criterion of success is the degree to which effective performance is adequate to the total amount of need.

4. *Cost Effectiveness.* This criterion is concerned with the evaluation of alternative methods in terms of costs; it represents a ratio between effort and impact.

5. *Process.* This "is not an inherent part of evaluative research" but rather an analysis of the process whereby a program produces the result it does; it is descriptive and diagnostic and looks for unanticipated negative and positive side-effects.

Different evaluation criteria will have a higher or lower priority among different levels of decision makers. Project and program managers are more likely to be concerned with *effort.* A program manager, however, should also be concerned with *effectiveness* and *process.* At higher agency levels, policy makers become more interested in questions of *impact* and *cost effectiveness.* Likewise, the different types of evaluation rely on different criteria:

project monitoring—effort

project rating—short-term measures of effectiveness

program strategy evaluation—effectiveness, process and cost effectiveness

program impact evaluation—effectiveness, impact and cost effectiveness.

Monitoring

Once a federal program is operational, it will be subject to monitoring—i.e., assessment of its ability to run. Most federal programs have this form of evaluation, if no other, although federal monitoring efforts are often severely limited by staffing constraints. Monitoring is the sphere of the auditing agency, the monitoring group, and the site visit. Attention is given to assessing *effort*—documentation of staff and activity of the program, documentation of expenditures, and examination of various "management indices" such as staff-client ratios, professional staff/supporting staff ratios, and unit costs of activities defined within the project's chart of accounts.

These are essentially input measures which have no necessary relationship with measures of output. As a result, most such measures turn out to be ambiguously interpretable. For example, relatively high average per diem hospital costs may be interpreted by auditors for reimbursement agencies as evidence of loose management practices, while they may be interpreted by professionally-oriented evaluators as indicators of "high-quality" hospitals. Because they have no necessary relationship with output measures (which have well-specified preference functions), there is a tendency for such systems to keep adding new items and become more and more cumbersome. As a result, writers on evaluation tend to look upon such activities as necessary evils, but boring, and "certainly not evaluation."

A major reason for present lack of knowledge of the relationships among inputs and outputs lies in the history of social program expansion in the last decade. As Cain and Hollister note (12), such programs

... often attempt to deliver services on a large enough scale to make a noticeable impact on the community and at the same time, they are expected to provide a quasi-experimental basis for determining what programs ought to be implemented and how they ought to be run.

If the mass installation of national programs were preceded by a "research and development" phase, then it would be possible, in theory, to determine the relationships between program inputs and outputs. Unfortunately, because R&D and mass operation phases tend to go on simultaneously in social programs (if there is an R&D operation at all), the needed research on the relationship between program inputs and outputs has usually not yet been done. To help overcome this failing in any large-scale program, the following questions should be used by officials to check program management:

> Has the program manager specified what the program is expected to produce, either in terms of single or multiple objectives?

> Does the program incorporate activities designed to determine whether the information derived from monitoring fairly reflects whether projects are reaching the stated objectives?

Follow-Up

A closely related problem facing evaluation studies is the question of follow-up. The relationship between short-term and long-term objectives is often unknown. Furthermore, in almost all the programs examined, the issue of the duration of program effects is important.

Program-wide studies cannot be completed overnight, but policy makers will continue to want and need "instant information" on program effectiveness. Evaluation study designs will have to provide for collection of data on groups who have received program services and on comparison groups over a period of time sufficient for possible program effects to appear or disappear—or for collection of reliable proxy indicators of long-term program effects. (As has been implied, one important use of field experiments and experimental demonstration projects mounted prior to start of an operating program would be to develop short-term and long-term output measures and, if possible, find short-term measures that will reliably predict longer-term effects.) Follow-up studies will usually be required for any definitive statements about the effectiveness of a program. Different programs will require different follow-up periods, but a period of less than a year or two will not be adequate for many programs.

The importance of follow-up data was brought out in the Borus five-year follow-up study of MDTA programs, in which average earnings gains *increased* during the five-year period. This study, which was based on use of Social Security data on earnings, suggested that MDTA has greater effects than were revealed by one- or two-year follow-up studies (8).

RECOMMENDATIONS–EFFECTIVENESS MEASURES

59. *Longitudinal Studies.* Federal evaluation funds generally should not be invested in program impact evaluation or program strategy evaluation studies that will yield only short-term measures of effectiveness. Consideration should be given to the collection of longitudinal data whenever feasible. (For example, studies of education programs yielding follow-up data over less than 12 months generally should not be funded, since at this point there is no reason to believe that fall-to-spring test score changes are particularly good measures of anything.)

60. *Research.* Evaluation funds ought to be invested, on a continuing basis, in basic research to establish and re-validate the usefulness of short-term output measures as predictors of the values of the longer-term output measures that are of ultimate real interest.

61. *Sampling.* For each major social program, agencies should examine the feasibility and potential usefulness of systems for collecting follow-up data on samples of program recipients for insights on the persistence or lack of persistence of program benefits. In many cases it will be desirable to assign follow-up work to outside contractors.

ISOLATION AND CONTROL OF TREATMENTS

One of the most challenging evaluation tasks, especially in evaluation of operating programs, is that of isolating and controlling treatments. The "ideal" evaluation will tell not only whether a program produces effects, but also what strategies or components of the program are most important to production of the effects. This section will consider the various types of evaluations and alternatives to evaluating on-going programs—field experiments and experimental demonstration projects—in terms of their ability to isolate and describe program strategies and the program itself.

Program Impact, Program Strategy, and Local Project Evaluation

Evaluation of an individual project is extremely difficult. If a single project is set up as a true experiment, with randomly chosen experimental and control groups, project performance can usually be measured. However, the results cannot be replicated with any confidence. Valid generalizations cannot be made because it will not be known whether the treatment can be replicated in other communities. For an individual local project, it is usually either very expensive or not feasible at all (because of a lack of controls or lack of methodology) to learn enough to say with confidence whether the project actually caused the effects measured.

Unfortunately, millions of federal dollars are being spent each year on noncomparable, unrelated evaluations of individual local projects (under Title I of the Elementary and Secondary Education Act, for example). Under present plans additional millions of federal dollars will be spent in the future on such evaluations (under the Model Cities program, for example). These noncomparable, unrelated evaluations of individual local projects, often done simply to satisfy federal evaluation requirements, are generally useful neither for national program planning nor for local program planning.

Instead, what we need are comparable evaluations of groups of projects attempting to deal with the same problem (e.g., educating black children of low-income families living in big-city ghettos). One can learn more from studies that use the same measures and the same methodology to compare what happened in several locations (especially if we choose locations where the projects are working in roughly the same type of environment, serving roughly the same kind of people). An important technique for improving the effectiveness of present levels of evaluation expenditures is, therefore, to pool the available evaluation resources into studies that allow the possibility of comparisons of the outputs of many projects in similar environments.

For *program impact evaluations*, Williams and Evans have suggested that equivalent national samples of those receiving and those not receiving treatment under the program can often be constructed on the basis of samples drawn from large numbers of communities (179, pp. 118-132). For example, Williams and Evans argue that the Westinghouse Learning Corporation-Ohio University evaluation of the Head Start program gives a reasonable picture of the average cognitive and motivational effects achieved through Head Start.

Williams argues further that evaluation of major program strategies can be accomplished in the same way as in a program impact evaluation, for example, comparing the relative effectiveness of a combination of on-the-job training and remedial reading vs. a combination of on-the-job training and counseling (178, pp. 454-458). In a study covering a large number of projects, the mitigating and unaccounted-for environmental and quality variables would average out and the evaluator would be more able to make valid generalizations for the program. Williams suggests, however, that precise evaluation of the effectiveness of more complex treatments within an operating program, especially evaluation that would tell *why* a particular local project worked, are beyond existing evaluation methodology. Beyond the level of reporting program participation/nonparticipation or the classification of individuals as having received services under major program components (e.g., on-the-job training, remedial reading, or counseling), the description of the treatment to which individuals have been exposed can be complex and very expensive.

Program strategy evaluation will often be difficult in an operating program, where inputs and organization of inputs are difficult to define and measure and where effects of program components will be intermingled, in unknown ways, with effects of other forces. Just how difficult and expensive program strategy evaluations can be is made clear by assessing the requirements for evaluating the relative effectiveness of different compensatory education program strategies: any analysis must take into account all major school programs, not just compensatory programs; must gather data on the social class of individual students, classrooms and schools; must use systematic and consistent testing; must describe programs in sufficient detail to allow identification of variations in inputs among grades and among schools; and must develop techniques for expenditure accounting by school and, if possible, by grade within schools (120). The collection and analysis of longitudinal data on very large numbers of children, together with required detailed description of the programs to which the children were exposed, make evaluation of compensatory education program strategies an expensive proposition.

Planned Variation

Often the environments in which programs operate will be so
complex, and the inputs to local projects so poorly defined, that
successful program strategy evaluation will either be impossible or
very difficult within the ongoing program. In many ongoing programs, the usefulness of program strategy evaluation will be
limited by one or more of the following conditions: (1) ongoing
programs may be too highly structured in one program model;
(2) treatments may be difficult or impossible to measure or to
distinguish from one another; and (3) in a non-experimental setting, it may be impossible to sort out the effects of environmental
and treatment variables.

Considering the cost and complexity of program strategy evaluation, the task of determining what components are most effective within a program will be more feasible if portions of a program can be operated as controlled experiments or if structural
variations can be introduced into portions of the program in
accord with an overall research design. In a number of programs, a
good deal could be learned if, say, 5 to 10 percent of program
funds (or corresponding amounts of demonstration grant monies)
were set aside for a program of "planned variation," consisting of
sets of experimental demonstration projects, each set developed
according to a single overall research design which includes an
overall evaluation design. The Office of Education Follow
Through program, for example, was redirected beginning in
1968-1969, changing from a typical unstructured demonstration
program (which extended Head Start staff and services into the
primary grades) to a highly structured program of "planned variation," designed to test the relative effectiveness of a number of
promising strategies for primary education of disadvantaged children. Each Follow Through strategy is being tested in a number of
communities with a common evaluation approach.

With "planned variation," we move from evaluation of ongoing
programs to alternatives to such evaluation—field experiments and
experimental demonstration projects, both defined in Chapter 2.
In such experimental programs, the evaluator exercises consider-
ably more control of inputs and processes than in ongoing programs and much less of the experimental design is sacrificed to
operational considerations.

In order to learn anything conclusive about the desirability of moving from small experimental projects to large-scale operating programs (or to major changes in existing operating programs), we need systematic investigation of the effects of major variations within the programs, under varying circumstances. Characteristics to be varied should be those that (a) are thought to be basic variables affecting program output and (b) are structural features of program organization, susceptible of implementation with relative consistency in a variety of situations.[32] Demonstration projects in most current federal programs do not come anywhere close to meeting the standards prescribed here—the federal government exercises little, if any, control over inputs or process and does little, if any, comparative evaluation of the relative effectiveness of different demonstration projects with similar objectives.

The New Jersey Negative Income Tax experiment is an example of the type of field experiment suggested here; the Office of Education Follow Through program, which evaluates a number of alternative approaches to primary education of disadvantaged children, also approximates the kind of experimental demonstration program suggested. A related strategy was to be pursued in the Department of Health, Education and Welfare (University of North Carolina) evaluation of family planning programs: there, *additional* services were to be experimentally introduced into operating programs, to test the effects of alternative strategies and techniques.

In the ideal world, field experiments and experimental demonstration projects would precede the operating programs to which they are related, furnishing indication of successful strategies, performance standards, and (if possible) useful short-term output measures; in the real world, such experimental projects will often have to be developed simultaneously with the operating program.

Project Rating

Up to now, the discussion has centered on evaluation which would assist decision makers in choosing among programs or major strat-

---

32. See *Child Development: Summary of the Child Development Task Force Report*, where such a program of planned variation was recommended for a number of programs, including the Follow Through program and pre-school and day care programs (153).

egies within programs. In this context, project by project evaluation may be unnecessarily costly. However, another set of decisions in most federal programs—those related to individual local projects—need to be addressed. The point has been made in the following manner:

> The development of PPB has, in most instances, been characterized by an almost exclusive concern with efforts to allocate resources optimally *among* programs. Very little attention, however, has focused on the problems of program management, i.e., the organization of resources *within* a program to achieve the greatest effect (5).

For many operating programs, evaluation of the relative effectiveness of different program strategies is too complicated or too expensive to be possible in the immediate future. With present deficiencies in evaluation methodology, we are usually unable to determine the relative importance of the various causal factors operating in a given locality. We may, however, have a fairly good idea of the most important environmental variables that would strongly influence the success or failure of local projects within a given program. If we could group local projects with similar objectives into classes within which the important environmental variables and type of population served are held constant, and if we could measure the outputs of the projects within a given class, then we would be able to assess the relative effectiveness of projects within a given class even without being able to define the functional relationships among environmental variables, treatment variables and outputs—and without paying the high price of collecting and analyzing process data on program components (treatments).

Bateman developed such a project rating system in HEW, to measure the relative efficiency and effectiveness of local projects within the Work Experience and Training Program (5). His system classified manpower projects according to area unemployment rates, proportion of male trainees and average age of trainees, and then compared the relative effectiveness of the training projects falling into each class. Using the trainee employment rate, occupational distribution, average wage and proportion entering advanced training as measures of project effectiveness, an aggregate index was developed to rank each project relative to others in its class. A project rating system is now being developed by a DOL-HEW contractor for the Work Incentive (WIN) program.[33]

Such project rating systems could provide the bases for incentive systems which would reward good project performance or penalize poor project performance, giving program administrators information that would be useful in efforts to upgrade their programs. Furthermore, such systems for classification of projects and rating of relative project outputs can provide the basis for subsequent program strategy evaluation designed to uncover the effects of different types of treatments within the program.

Evaluation-Related Activities

When determining appropriate methodology for evaluations, explicit account should be taken of evaluation-related activities—monitoring, cost analysis and reporting systems (see Chapter 2 for definitions).

Program managers and regional office staffs can be encouraged to include assessment of project output as part of their monitoring operations. On the basis of short-term or intermediate output measures, relative performance of different projects may be assessed. This will help identify projects that are successful, those which are in difficulty and those which ought to be terminated.

Cost analysis often can throw a good deal of light on a program even when effects are hard or impossible to measure. For example, in the delivery of health or legal services it is frequently difficult to measure benefits, but a comparative analysis of project costs would provide program managers with valuable information for decision making and program control.

Reporting systems to provide basic information about services provided, characteristics of the population receiving services and the experience of recipients is essential to policy makers and program managers. Good evaluation relies on this. Yet federal agency utilization of information systems for program management and evaluation is poor. Some agencies have information systems, but the products of these systems were found to be not usable or not

---

33. See DOL RFP, "Specifications for Proposal of Contracts for (1) An Impact Evaluation of the Work Incentive Program (WIN) and (2) A Rating System for WIN Projects," 1970.

used. In other agencies, programs are being managed and evaluated without benefit of any formal information system. One of the largest and most conspicuously unutilized reporting systems has been OEO's CAP Management Information System (MIS). Although pilot tested and "proven feasible" by 68 community action agencies, MIS was acknowledged as a failure by OEO officials. The reasons given for this are worth detailing because they raise questions that are instructive for the design of other reporting systems.

MIS was complex. It lacked the investment and expertise at the local level for proper collecting, recording and compiling, so data received was incomplete or inaccurate. There was no mechanism for reviewing the local system. Target populations, hostile to studies and surveys, gave strong resistance to many information collection efforts. Utility of the data collected was limited because it usually measured "volume of business" rather than program output (either in terms of national objectives or local aims). Some considered MIS unrealistic or overambitious in attempting to provide data both for program operation and for evaluation. In sum, because MIS fell into disrepute, people were reluctant to use even such information as it provided.

Personnel in state and local agencies and local projects have rarely been interested in reporting to federal agencies, especially if the data are of little relevance to state or local needs. As the states take on increased program responsibilities and therefore need more information for their own policy and operational decisions, their sympathy for federal reporting requirements may grow. In cooperating with 27 states, for example, the Office of Education is now developing a unified system for state and local reporting that will, on the basis of valid statistical samples, provide data on services and characteristics of children and schools served under several Office of Education elementary and secondary education programs, the costs of the services provided, and estimates of the children's achievement after they receive services.

RECOMMENDATIONS–ISOLATION AND CONTROL OF TREATMENTS

62. *Planned Variation.* Managers of operating programs should be given responsibility for introducing planned variations and pos-

sibly even controlled experiments into a small portion of their operating program or into a related experimental demonstration program. Especially in those federal operating programs in which decisions on project operation are very decentralized, such as Title I of the Elementary and Secondary Education Act, the relative value of alternative strategies and techniques can often be best assessed through planned variations and comparable evaluations.

63. *Funds for Experimentation.* A portion of program funds—probably in the range of 5 to 10 percent—should be devoted to field experiments (with control groups, etc.), and systematically designed experimental demonstration projects.

64. *Congressional Support.* For major programs not having authority or funds to mount experimental demonstration projects, the administration should seek the necessary authorities and funds from Congress.

65. *Relating Achievements to Goals.* Since, except in controlled experiments, evaluation of individual local projects will often be beyond present methodology or outside reasonable cost constraints, single-project evaluations should be steered toward comparison of project achievements with objectives as previously stated in measurable terms.

66. *Rating Systems.* To assist internal program decision making and to serve as a basis for dissemination of information on "best practices," program managers should attempt to develop output-oriented project classification and rating systems that could, as a minimum goal, pick out the top 10 to 25 percent and bottom 10 to 25 percent of each class of projects that have similar objectives, serve similar populations and operate in similar environments. Since project rating will usually be more feasible and less costly than program strategy evaluation, operating-level evaluation staffs should consider development and use of project rating systems as initial steps prior to undertaking the more "ideal" program strategy evaluations (which would attempt to tell you not only *what* happened but also *why*).

67. *Monitoring.* Program managers should be encouraged to tie project rating systems to their monitoring operations and to relate questions of project outputs to questions of administrative efficiency.

68. *Balanced View.* Planned variations and project rating systems should supplement program impact evaluations to help ensure that

useful approaches will not be discredited by overall program failure, and that wasteful or ineffective practices will not be concealed by overall program success.

69. *Incentives.* Federal, state and local program managers should
use rating as one basis for incentive systems that reward outstanding local projects.

70. *Reporting System.* For each major social program, agencies
should examine the feasibility and potential usefulness of developing a reporting system—possibly based on random sampling of
recipients—that provides basic information on characteristics of
the population served and the services offered.

71. *Costs.* Cost analysis of program and project costs should be
considered as an adjunct to all types of evaluations, and is particularly valuable when program effects are difficult or impossible to
evaluate.

FEASIBILITY OF EVALUATION

If the recent past has witnessed almost no scientific evaluation of
federal social programs, it would be equally erroneous to suppose
now that almost every federal activity lends itself to useful evaluation. Many programs, and many local projects or strategies within
programs, do not.

An essential first condition for evaluating a program's impact is
the existence of methods to distinguish between effects of the
program and the effects of other forces—in short, the ability to
isolate what would have happened in the absence of the program.
At best, evaluating most social programs is complex and difficult.

In general, evaluation will be more feasible if program inputs are
tightly controlled—in a situation approximating an experimental
design—or if program inputs can reasonably be expected to have
large effects relative to the effects of other forces at work.

Major factors determining the feasibility of evaluating a federal
program include the following:

The type of evaluation desired.

The existence of applicable theory and methods.

The time and money available.

The availability and accessibility of suitable comparison groups.

The ability to collect required data.

Table 5 indicates the conditions under which different types of evaluation will be theoretically feasible. From a methodological standpoint, the feasibility of the various types of evaluation depends on the availability of suitable measures of effectiveness, which may or may not exist for given programs. Program impact evaluation will usually be methodologically feasible, although it may be impossible to isolate the effects of federal inputs from the effects of state and local inputs. Project rating will often be feasible; the main problem, however, will be to devise suitable systems for classifying the environments within which projects are operating. Local project evaluation and program strategy evaluation are the most difficult and most costly; they are often beyond the capabilities of existing methodology, except in situations resembling controlled experiments.

Evaluation staffs, before investing funds and launching studies, should carefully analyze whether proposed evaluations are feasible. Considerations of feasibility, as related to the specific types of evaluation, are as follows:

Program impact evaluation. From a methodological standpoint, program impact evaluation depends on the availability of suitable output measures and appropriate comparison groups, or time-series data. Unless federal inputs are large relative to state and local inputs, however, it may be impossible to isolate the impact

Table 5. Methodological Feasibility of Evaluation

Program Impact Evaluation and Local Project Evaluation	Project Rating	Program Strategy Evaluation
Feasible given availability of suitable *output measures* and appropriate *comparison* groups[a].	Feasible given availability of suitable *output measures* and *measures of appropriate characteristics of project participants and of the social and economic environments in which projects operate.* These characteristics (e.g., race, family income, area unemployment rate) will be selected on the basis of suitable analytic models. In most cases, it will make sense to rate projects against one another only if they are operating in similar environments.	Feasible given availability of suitable *output measures; measures of appropriate characteristics of project participants and of the social and economic environment in which projects operate; measures of appropriate input and process variables; and wide variations in program strategies and techniques.* The characteristics of environment, input, and process variables (e.g., type training, type follow-up services provided) will be selected on the basis of suitable analytic models.

[a] The overall effectiveness of the *federal* share of a national program can be evaluated only if the federal funding is a significant portion of the total or if the federal program is operated as a controlled experiment.

of a national federal program—or one of its local projects—on a population receiving services from several sources.

In the interest of greater feasibility, two kinds of program impact studies should be distinguished in development of evaluation plans: studies of the effectiveness of a single national program, and comparative studies of the costs and effectiveness of two or more national programs in achieving common objectives. Because policy questions typically focus on what program is better, and not whether there should be a program in a given problem area, comparative studies are preferable for producing significant and useful findings.

Program impact evaluation is probably feasible for all the programs examined, with the possible exception of very complex programs like the Community Action Program, Urban Renewal, and the Model Cities program. See Table 6 for considerations involved in estimating conditions for the successful evaluation of a number of the programs examined in this study.

Program strategy evaluation. Program strategy evaluation will be the most difficult and costly type to undertake in an operating program. This is especially the case when project inputs are hard to define and measure or when effects of alternative strategies and techniques are intermingled in unknown ways with the effects of other forces. The task of determining what strategies and techniques are most effective within a program will be more feasible for programs operated as controlled experiments and for programs in which major structural variations are introduced according to an overall research design. Program strategy evaluation is most feasible for manpower programs, family planning programs, and tightly controlled or heavily funded education programs. Table 6 indicates the methodological reasons leading to these conclusions.

Local project evaluation. Local evaluation of an individual project is usually not feasible unless the project was developed as a field experiment, since the appropriate comparison of effects with and without the project will not be possible. For any single project, it is usually impossible or too costly to learn enough to say with confidence whether the project—or other forces—actually caused the effects measured.

Unfortunately, millions of federal dollars are being spent each year on individual evaluations of local projects under Title I of the Elementary and Secondary Education Act. Additional millions of

Table 6. Preliminary Estimates on Existence of Conditions for Evaluation
of Selected Federal Programs

Code: +: Existing methodology is sufficient and readily available for immediate application to evaluation.
       0: Methodology is not advanced and application cannot be made with complete confidence. Development of
           methodology will be a critical part of the evaluation.
       -: Methodology unavailable. Development of an applicable method appeared unlikely at this time.

Program	Agency	Availability of Suitable Output Measures[a]	Availability of Measures of Appropriate Environmental Variables[b]	Availability of Appropriate Comparison Groups[c]	Availability of Measures of Appropriate Input and Process Variables[d]
Manpower Development and Training Programs	DOL	+	0	0	+
Neighborhood Youth Corps (NYC)	DOL/OEO	+	0	0	+
Job Opportunities in the Business Sector (JOBS)	DOL	+	0	0	+
Work Incentive Program (WIN)	DOL/HEW	+	0	0	+
Maternal and Child Health Programs					
Maternal and Child Health Services	HEW	0	+	0	0
Crippled Children's Services	HEW	+	+	+	+
Maternity and Infant Care Project	HEW	+	+	+	+
Comprehensive Health Care for Children and Youth	HEW	0	+	+	0
Family Planning	HEW/OEO	+	+	+	+
Vocational Education	HEW	+	0	-	0
Title I, Elementary and Secondary Education Act	HEW	0	+	-	0
Follow Through	HEW	0	+	+	0
Job Corps	OEO/DOL	+	0	0	+
Head Start	OEO/HEW	0	+	-	0
Legal Services Program	OEO	0	0	+	0
Community Action Program	OEO	0	0	-	0
Urban Renewal	HUD	0	0	0	0
Model Cities ·	HUD	0	0	0	0

[a]Necessary for national program impact evaluation, for local project evaluation, for project rating, and for program strategy evaluation.
[b]Necessary for project rating and program strategy evaluation.
[c]Necessary for program impact evaluation.
[d]Necessary for program strategy evaluation.

federal dollars may be spent in the future on evaluation of individual Model Cities projects. Federal evaluation funds generally
should not be allocated to elaborate evaluations of individual
projects. Evaluations of individual projects should generally focus

on relatively inexpensive short-term assessments of the extent to which performance objectives have been attained or the extent to which baseline conditions have been changed.

An important technique for improving the effectiveness of present levels of evaluation expenditures is to pool the evaluation funds into large studies that compare the results of projects in several locations. Evaluation has to involve comparison. More can be learned from studies that use the same methodology to compare what happened in several locations, especially if several sets of locations are chosen so that, within each set, the program is working in the same type of environment with the same kinds of recipients of services. For programs where most decisions are made at state and local levels, federal evaluation funds and technical assistance should be channeled to groups of cooperating states or localities that share similar problems and are willing to undertake comparable evaluations from which each can learn.

Some type of program or project *monitoring* is always feasible through site visits. An important methodological problem, however, is the development of monitoring systems that will (1) make possible reliable comparisons among projects and (2) direct attention to (at least short-term) project outputs.

Project rating. Project rating will usually be more feasible and less costly than program strategy evaluation.

Data collection. Evaluation feasibility obviously relies heavily on the availability of significant and reliable data. Yet program reporting systems generally have proven ineffective in generating required input data.

RECOMMENDATION—FEASIBILITY

72. Before investing funds in evaluation studies, agency-level and operating-level evaluation staffs should perform analyses of methodological and practical feasibility, based on type of evaluation desired, stage of development of theory and measures suitable for the evaluation desired, time available for evaluation, availability of suitable comparison groups, and feasibility of collecting the required data on program participants and members of appropriate comparison groups.

7. Summary of Major Recommendations

This section lists the major recommendations with regard to federal evaluation policy that have emerged from this study. These recommendations are presented according to the government levels that would be directly responsible for their implementation: the Executive Office, Congress, federal agencies and individual program offices. The evaluation role of the states and localities is discussed in terms of their relationship to the federal agencies.

(These summary recommendations duplicate or parallel many of those found elsewhere under topic headings. To avoid confusion, those in earlier chapters are numbered 1 through 72, while summary recommendations are numbered S1 through S34.)

ROLE OF THE EXECUTIVE OFFICE

The Executive Office plays a critical role in the evaluation process. It must provide leadership, set priorities among studies and establish a federal evaluation system.

Leadership

S1. The President should continue to emphasize to federal agencies his determination to require and use objective evidence of program effectiveness in drawing up the Administration's budget and legislative program.

Priorities

S2. Both the Council for Urban Affairs and the Bureau of the Budget periodically should state the major questions on the effectiveness and appropriateness of existing programs that face the Executive Office.[34]

Federal Evaluation System

S3. The federal government needs a system that provides timely answers to major questions on the effectiveness and appropriateness of existing programs. The Bureau of the Budget should develop such a system. To do so it must have the resources and authority to require, review and approve agency evaluation plans, to prepare overall federal evaluation plans, and to undertake evaluation studies itself.

To accomplish these tasks, the Budget Bureau should first require each federal agency to submit, as part of its annual budget justification, a two- to three-year plan for evaluating each of its major programs.

Second, on the basis of these agency plans and inputs from the White House and Council for Urban Affairs, the Budget Bureau should prepare annually its own comprehensive two- to three-year evaluation plan. For each major federal program (or set of related programs) the plan should show the national program impact and program strategy evaluations required and under way; the questions to be answered and by what dates; and the major assumptions and measures to be used. The Bureau's evaluation staff, in preparing the plan, should solicit the BOB examining divisions and the agencies for indications of priorities and timing requirements.

Third, through the Bureau of the Budget, the President should require initiation of (1) national program impact evaluations that cross agency lines to compare the effectiveness of related programs in achieving common objectives and (2) evaluations of how different federal programs can be used together to create effective local programs. The Bureau of the Budget should attempt to have such evaluation studies accomplished through cooperative efforts of the agencies concerned. If the agencies concerned are unable or unwill-

---

34. See note 20, page 58 above.

ing to undertake high priority interagency evaluations of these kinds, the Bureau of the Budget should be given the resources to accomplish the required studies.

A budget on the order of $3 million per year and six staff members should be provided for Bureau of the Budget evaluation activities.

Requests for Resources

S4. To give life to an evaluation system, the Administration should request the necessary evaluation staff and funds from Congress for the Bureau of the Budget, agencies and operating organizations. The President also should encourage Cabinet officials to allocate existing staff and money to major evaluation efforts.

ROLE OF THE CONGRESS

Congress, as one of the primary users of evaluation studies, has a large stake in the active support and guidance of a federal evaluation system.

National Impact Evaluations

S5. Congress should require, every two to three years, program impact evaluations of each major federal program. When appropriate, Congress should specify that such studies be based on follow-up of samples of program participants and members of relevant comparison groups. These evaluations should be done at a level removed from direct control of the program manager—at department level, in the Bureau of the Budget or in an office directly responsible to Congress. Congress should provide funds and staff to design, supervise, execute and disseminate these evaluation studies.

Program Strategy Evaluation

S6. Congress should make available, in each major program, funds and staff for program strategy evaluation (unless the studies would not be expected to be worth the cost). In particular, in each demonstration or pilot program, Congress should require a statement of the projects planned and a description of the system to be used for comparing the relative effectiveness of the different strategies and techniques to be tested.

ROLE OF THE FEDERAL AGENCIES

The responsibilities of a federal agency can be broadly categorized as follows: definition of program objectives, development of agency-wide evaluation work plans, carrying out comprehensive evaluation efforts, and dissemination and use of evaluation studies. The agency head must provide official support and assign responsibility and resources among various agency offices.

Agency Head Support

S7. Each department head should establish an evaluation system with adequate staff and money to measure the effectiveness of major agency programs. Evaluation results should be required in the drawing up of budgets and legislative proposals.

S8. Agency heads should require program managers to conduct the evaluation activities necessary to operate their programs effectively and efficiently.

Evaluation Plan

S9. At the beginning of each fiscal year, each agency should develop or update a two- to three-year evaluation work plan stating which studies are in progress and which are projected. Approval of this plan should be required at the beginning of each fiscal year as a condition for authority to spend evaluation funds. This plan should be prepared by the agency-level evaluation staff in cooperation with policy makers, budget staffs, program managers and operating-level evaluation staffs. Evaluation planning is a continual process: when the agency appropriation is known, the evaluation plan should be reassessed in light of firm budget figures.

S10. Since useful evaluation studies are likely to be costly, agencies should place emphasis on *feasible* studies of *major* programs where the value of the findings would outweigh the costs.

S11. For each of the agency's major programs or groups of related programs, the agency work plans should address the question of priorities among the following tasks:

a. program impact evaluation

b. program strategy evaluation

c. field experiments and experimental demonstration projects

d. project rating

e. local project evaluation

f. monitoring

g. routine reporting

h. cost analysis

i. development of evaluation methodology

j. development and demonstration of incentive systems that would reward project managers for productivity.

Types of Evaluation

S12. In development of work plans, two kinds of program impact studies should be considered, those that assess a *single* national program, and *comparative* studies of two or more national programs with common objectives. Because budget decisions frequently can be aided by knowing what program is better, comparative evaluations should be given precedence whenever feasible.

S13. Program impact evaluations to measure average national effectiveness should be supplemented, to the extent possible, by project rating systems and program strategy evaluations, or related field experiments and experimental demonstrations. These steps will help ensure that useful approaches will not be discredited by overall program failure, nor wasteful practices concealed by overall program success.

S14. Agencies should shift federal resources away from elaborate, noncomparable evaluations of individual local projects to project rating, national program impact evaluation and program strategy evaluation.

S15. Evaluation staffs should pay particular attention to the possibility of using experimental demonstration projects to test the effectiveness of different program strategies.

S16. Agency-level evaluation staffs should assist program managers and their staffs in Washington, regional offices, states and local agencies to clarify objectives, develop project rating systems, identify the relatively successful and unsuccessful projects, and generally upgrade the average quality of their programs.

S17. Federal agencies should develop incentive systems at federal, state or local levels to reward outstanding performance by local projects.

Methodology

S18. Evaluation staffs should put heavy emphasis on methodology, particularly on the development of (a) valid short-term and long-term indicators of effectiveness, (b) systems for assessing the relative effectiveness of comparable local projects, and (c) standard systems for comparing project costs.

S19. Agency-level evaluation staffs should plan and carry out studies designed to determine how the introduction and use of output measures that capture only a portion of program goals affect the direction of the program. (For instance, will program directors shift major emphasis to whatever is being measured and ignore other important activities?)

Organizational Responsibilities

S20. Responsibility for evaluation should be placed at a level appropriate to the decisions it is designed to assist. Department or agency heads should assign major evaluation responsibilities on the basis that, to the extent possible, evaluations should be directed by persons not having a great deal to gain or lose from the outcome. Thus, a member of a program staff should not have to judge whether his program is worth having, or whether the program manager is performing adequately. Major responsibilities for evaluating projects and alternative strategies *within* the program should rest with operating bureau chiefs and program managers, but responsibility for evaluating the worth of an entire program should be placed above the program level.

S21. For programs such as education to which state and local governments contribute major shares of support and in which decisions are made mostly at state and local levels, federal evaluation funds and technical assistance should be channeled to groups of cooperating states or groups of cooperating localities to obtain comparable studies.

S22. For such programs, agencies should rely heavily on program strategy evaluation in conjunction with field experiments or experimental demonstration programs. Agencies should also develop and demonstrate project rating systems for state and local use. Whenever its funds are expended, the federal government should retain some evaluation role to discharge its duty to administer public funds efficiently.

S23. In a large number of program areas, federal, state, and local governments should work together to establish cooperative mechanisms for objective evaluation of alternative program strategies. These cooperative efforts should provide for systematic examination of major program variations; for the collection of comparable data on costs, process and outputs; and for the collection of follow-up data to compare the impact of different approaches.

Funding

S24. Agency heads should order a review of each major social program to determine (a) what funds are available for evaluating that program, (b) how the funds are allocated among different types of evaluation, and (c) what level of evaluation funding would be reasonable. When indicated on the basis of this review, the Administration should have legislation introduced to allow the agency head to set aside for evaluation a relatively small percentage of program funds (probably in the range from one-half to two percent).

Staff

S25. Full-time evaluation staffs should be created at department/ agency and operating bureau/program levels, with major efforts to attract highly qualified professionals. Positions from existing planning and research staffs should be allocated to evaluation.

S26. Evaluation staffs should include as a bare minimum at least one professional for every two to four ongoing evaluation studies, or for every $500,000 worth of ongoing studies done under contracts or grants. Beyond the staff required to carry out the relatively small number of studies undertaken in any one year, additional staff are needed to pursue the many other evaluation functions: developing work plans, helping define program objectives and output measures, and developing methodology.

S27. Since some of the most challenging tasks—program strategy evaluation, project rating and designing experiments and experimental demonstration projects—will most appropriately be accomplished at the bureau/operating program level, agency heads should resist the tendency to reserve high grade-level positions only for the department/agency level.

S28. Agencies faced with strict constraints on in-house staff positions should consider use of contractors to assist in the design of evaluation studies, including preparation of work statements to be used in Requests for Proposals, recognizing that significant though smaller amounts of in-house staff time will still be required.

ROLE OF PROGRAM OFFICES

Program managers and operating personnel have three roles: (1) ensuring that projects they administer carry out the stated program objectives, (2) testing different approaches to achieve program goals, and (3) communicating the results of their findings on program effectiveness to the appropriate policy makers and program directors.

Administration of Evaluation

S29. Each operating bureau and program manager should be responsible for seeing that evidence is produced on the relative effectiveness of different projects or program strategies within each major program. Major operating bureaus (and in some cases, individual programs) should establish evaluation divisions to: (1) develop two- to three-year work plans to be included in the agency evaluation plan; (2) help program managers define program objectives in measurable terms; (3) conduct program strategy and project rating evaluations; (4) help design field experiments and experimental demonstration projects, and (5) disseminate the results of significant evaluation studies to program managers and policy makers at relevant federal, state and local levels.

S30. Because of existing limitations on in-house evaluation staff time and expertise, program managers should consider contracting for help in planning evaluation studies, field experiments and experimental demonstration projects.

Types of Evaluation

S31. To assist internal program decision-making and to serve as a basis for dissemination of information on "best practices," program managers should attempt to develop output-oriented project classification and rating systems that could, as a minimum, pick out the top 10-25 percent and the bottom 10-25 percent of each class of projects that have similar objectives, serve similar populations and operate in similar environments. For programs in which decision-making authority is delegated to federal regional offices, these offices should be given responsibility of rating the relative project effectiveness within groups of comparable projects in their region.

S32. Program managers and regional office staffs should attempt to include in their monitoring operations the assessment of project output—in particular, assessment of relative outputs of comparable projects.

S33. In order to test the relative effectiveness of different strategies and techniques within their programs, managers should whenever possible devote a portion of their funds to field experiments and experimental demonstration projects.

S34. Since (except in the case of controlled experiments) evaluation of the effectiveness of individual local projects will often be beyond present methodology or outside reasonable cost constraints, single-project evaluations should be steered toward periodic comparison of project outputs with objectives previously stated in measurable terms.

Select Bibliography

1. The American Institute for Research in the Behavioral Sciences. *The AIR Study. A Study of Selected Exemplary Programs for the Education of Disadvantaged Children.* Palo Alto, California: September 1968.

2. Anderson, Martin. *The Federal Bulldozer: A Critical Analysis of Urban Renewal, 1949-1962.* Cambridge: Massachusetts Institute of Technology Press, 1964.

3. Abt Associates Inc. *A Study of The Neighborhood Center.* Pilot Program. Prepared for the Executive Office of the President, Bureau of the Budget, Cambridge: April 30, 1969.

4. Basic Systems, Inc. *Evaluation System for Community Action Programs.* Prepared for the Office of Economic Opportunity. New York: February 28, 1966.

5. Bateman, Worth. "Assessing Program Effectiveness: A Rating System for Identifying Relative Project Success," *Welfare in Review,* January-February 1968.

6. Bauer, Raymond, ed. *Social Indicators,* Cambridge: The Massachusetts Institute of Technology Press, 1966.

7. Baxter, McDonald & Co. *Budgeting and Evaluating Community Action Programs.* Prepared for the Office of Economic Opportunity. Berkeley: February 1968.

8. Borus, Michael E. "A Benefit-Cost Analysis of the Economic Effectiveness of Retraining the Unemployed," *Yale Economic Essays,* vol. 4, no. 2, Fall 1964.

9. Boyce, David E. and Day, Norman D. *Metropolitan Plan Evaluation Methodology.* Philadelphia: Institute for Environmental Studies, University of Pennsylvania, March 1969.

10. Buenaventura, Angeles. *Follow-Up Study of MDTA E&D Project Conducted by the Michigan Catholic Conference, Lansing*. Washington: Bureau of Social Science Research, March 1967.

11. Cain, Glen G. *Benefit/Cost Estimates for Job Corps*. Madison: Institute for Research on Poverty, University of Wisconsin, 1967.

12. _____. and Hollister, Robinson G. "Evaluating Manpower Programs for the Disadvantaged." Paper delivered at the North American Conference on Cost-Benefit Analysis of Manpower Programs, May 1969.

13. _____. *Methods for Evaluating Manpower Programs*. Madison: Institute for Research on Poverty, University of Wisconsin.

14. Campbell, D. T. and Stanley, J. C. *Experimental and Quasi-Experimental Designs for Research*. Chicago: Rand McNally, 1963.

15. Chamber of Commerce of the United States. *Youth and the War on Poverty*. An evaluation of the Job Corps, Neighborhood Youth Corps, and Project Head Start. Washington, D.C.

16. Chase, Samuel B., Jr., ed. *Problems in Public Expenditure Analysis*. Washington: The Brookings Institution, 1968.

17. Clark, T. N. "Community Structure, Decision-Making, Budget Expenditures, and Urban Renewal in 51 American Communities," *American Sociological Review*, August 1968.

18. Cleaveland, Frederic N. *Congress and Urban Problems*. Washington: The Brookings Institution, 1968.

19. Comptroller General of the United States. *Review of Economic Opportunity Programs, Report to the Congress of the United States*. Washington: Government Printing Office, March 1969.

20. Consad Research Corp. *CAP Impact Model*. Prepared for the Office of Economic Opportunity. Presents a model for measuring effectiveness of CAP in low-income urban areas. Pittsburgh: June 1968.

21. Curran, Barbara A. *Interim Report: Research Study to Assess the Need for the Utilization of Legal Services by the Poor*. Chicago: American Bar Foundation, December 1968.

22. Dalton, Melville and Glass, John F. *An Observational Analysis Study of Los Angeles Neighborhood Youth Corps Projects*. Los Angeles: Department of Sociology, University of California, 1968.

23. Deniston, O. L., Rosenstock, I. M., and Getting, V. A. "Evaluation of Program Effectiveness," *Public Health Reports*, April 1968.

24. Don Vito, P. A. *Annotated Bibliography on Systems Cost Analysis*. Santa Monica: The Rand Corp., March 1967.

25. Dorfman, Robert. *Measuring Benefits of Government Investments.* Papers presented at a conference of experts held in Washington, D. C. on November 7-9, 1963. Washington: The Brookings Institution, 1965.

26. Dunlap and Associates, Inc. *Evaluation of Neighborhood Youth Corps Projects.* OEO 916. Darien: February 1966.

27. Education Systems Research Institute. *The Process and Product of T. I. High School Level Vocational Education in the United States.* Pittsburgh: April 1968.

28. Estes, Nolan. "ESEA: Its Promise, Accomplishments, and Problems," *National Association of Secondary School Principals Bulletin*, May 1968.

29. Evans, John. "Evaluation of OEO Programs," unpublished memo. Office of Research, Plans, Programs and Evaluation, Office of Economic Opportunity, April 15, 1969.

30. Freeman, (Cole) & Associates, Inc. *Manual for Evaluating Approved VISTA Projects*, Part II. Prepared for the Office of Economic Opportunity. Washington: December 15, 1967.

31. _____. *Manual for Evaluating VISTA Project Proposals*, Part III. Prepared for the Office of Economic Opportunity. Washington: December 15, 1968.

32. _____. *A Procedure for Evaluating VISTA Project Effectiveness*, Part I. Prepared for the Office of Economic Opportunity. Washington: December 15, 1967.

33. French, Curin, et al. *A National Attitude Survey of MDTA Trainees.* In preparation at University of Michigan for Office of Research, Manpower Administration; 2,000 personal interviews and 4,000 questionnaires. Preliminary paper, August 1968.

34. Frieden, Bernard and Morris, R. *Urban Planning and Social Policy.* New York: Basic Books, 1968.

35. Gans, Herbert J. "The Failure of Urban Renewal: A Critique and Some Proposals," *Commentary*, April 1965.

36. General Electric Co. Tempo Division. *Survey and Analyses of Results from Title I Funding for Compensatory Education.* A report prepared for the Department of Health, Education and Welfare. Santa Barbara: 1968.

37. Glennan, Thomas K., Jr. *Evaluating Federal Manpower Programs: Notes and Observations.* Rand Corp. Memorandum, RM-5743-OEO. Santa Monica: September 1969.

38. Goldston, Eli, Hunter, Allan O., and Rothrauff, Guido A., Jr. "Urban Redevelopment—The Viewpoint of Counsel for a Private Redeveloper," *Law and Contemporary Problems*, Winter 1961.

39. Graae, Steffen. *Evaluating OEO Programs*. Internal OEO document. December 1968.

40. Greenberg, D. H. *Employers and Manpower Training Programs: Data Collection and Analysis*. Prepared for the Office of Economic Opportunity. Santa Monica: The Rand Corp., October 1968.

41. Greer, Scott. *Urban Renewal and American Cities; the Dilemma of Democratic Intervention*. Indianapolis: Bobbs-Merrill, 1965.

42. Groberg, Robert P. "Urban Renewal Realistically Reappraised," *Law and Contemporary Problems*, Winter 1965.

43. Guba, Egon G. *Development, Diffusion, and Evaluation*. Bloomington, Indiana: The National Institute for the Study of Educational Change, October 1967.

44. _____. *Evaluation and Change in Education*. Bloomington, Indiana: The National Institute for the Study of Educational Change, May 1968.

45. Hammer, Green, Siler Associates. *Planning Effectiveness and 701: An Evaluation*. Washington: October 1967.

46. Hansen, W. Lee, Weisbrod, Burton A., and Scanlon, William. *Determinants of Income: Does Schooling Really Count?* Madison: University of Wisconsin, 1967.

47. Harris (Louis) and Associates, Inc. *A Survey of Ex-Job Corpsmen*. Study Number 1899, New York: April 1969.

48. Harsh, J. R. "Evaluating ESEA Projects for the Disadvantaged," *Educational Leadership*, February 1967.

49. Hess, Robert D. and Tapp, Jane L. *An Evaluation of the Effectiveness of a Community Based Manpower Training Program*. Chicago: University of Chicago, 1967.

50. Hoffman, N. March. *Follow-Up Study of MDTA E&D Project at Bluefield State College*. Washington: Bureau of Social Science Research, Inc., May 1967.

51. Hudson Institute, Inc. *The Future of American Poverty: Some Basic Issues in Evaluating Alternative Anti-Poverty Measures*. Croton-on-Hudson, New York: April 1968.

52. Human Interaction Research Institute. *Operation Retrieval, Impact on Community Organizations and Institutes Made by MDTA Experimental and Demonstration Projects for Disadvantaged Youth*. Prepared for Department of Labor, Office of Manpower Policy, Evaluation and Research. Los Angeles: June 1967.

53. _____. *Putting Research, Experimental and Demonstration Findings to Use*. Prepared for the U. S. Department of Labor. Washington: June 1967.

54. Hunter, William G. and Kittrell, J. R. "Evolutionary Operation: A Review," *Technometrics*, Vol. 8, No. 3, August 1966.

55. Institute for Educational Development. *A Digest of the Research Activities of Regional Evaluation and Research Centers for Project Head Start, 1966-1967*. Prepared for the Office of Economic Opportunity. Washington: January 15, 1968.

56. Jakubauskas, Edward B. and Baumel, C. Phillip, eds. *Human Resources Development*. Ames, Iowa: The Iowa State University Press, 1967.

57. Job Corps, "Research and Evaluation, Job Corps Benefit/Cost Analysis, September 1968." Washington: Office of Economic Opportunity, Job Corps, 1968.

58. Kirschner Associates. *A Description and Evaluation of Selected Educational Components of Community Action Programs*. Prepared for the Office of Economic Opportunity. Albuquerque: May 1967.

59. _____. *Description and Evaluation of Neighborhood Centers*. Prepared for the Office of Economic Opportunity. Albuquerque: November 15, 1966.

60. _____. *Description and Evaluation of Neighborhood Centers*. Prepared for the Office of Economic Opportunity. Albuquerque: December 1966.

61. Krutilla, J. V. "Welfare Aspects of Benefit-Cost Analysis," *Journal of Political Economy*, June 1961.

62. Leach, Richard H. *Cost-Benefit Analysis in Urban Redevelopment*. Real Estate Research Program, Institute of Business and Economic Research. Berkeley: University of California, 1962.

63. _____. "The Federal Urban Renewal Program: A Ten-Year Critique," *Law and Contemporary Problems*, Autumn 1960.

64. Levin, Henry M. *Cost-Effectiveness Analysis and Educational Policy—Profusion, Confusion, Promise*. Stanford: Stanford Center for Research and Development in Teaching, Stanford University, December 1968.

65. Levine, Abraham S. "Cost-Benefit Analysis and Social Welfare Program Evaluation," *Social Service Review*, June 1968.

66. Levinson, Perry. "Evaluation of Social Welfare Programs, Two Research Models," *Welfare in Review*, December 1966.

67. _____. and Mangum, Garth L. *Making Sense of Federal Manpower Policy* (Policy Papers in Human Resources and Industrial Relations, No. 2). Ann

Arbor: The Institute of Labor and Industrial Relations, University of Michigan and Wayne State University, March 1967.

68. Little (Arthur D.), Inc. *Local Planning: Performance and Expectations.* Study contracted by the Department of Housing and Urban Development. Cambridge, Massachusetts: September 1967.

69. Logan, James. "CAA Evaluation Manual," cited in *Evaluation of the War on Poverty, Status and Prospects at OEO.* Prepared for General Accounting Office. Bethesda, Maryland: Resource Management Corp., 1969.

70. London, H. H. *How Fare MDTA Ex-Trainees?* Prepared for Office of Manpower Policy, Evaluation and Research. Columbia, Missouri: University of Missouri, December 1967.

71. Main, Earl D. "A Nationwide Evaluation of MDTA Institutional Job Training," *Journal of Human Resources*, Spring 1968.

72. Mangum, Garth L. *Contributions and Cost of Manpower Development and Training* (Policy Papers in Human Resources and Industrial Relations, No. 5). Ann Arbor: Institute of Labor and Industrial Relations, University of Michigan and Wayne State University, December 1967.

73. _____. "Evaluating Federal Manpower Programs," *Employment and Training Legislation–1968*, prepared for the Subcommittee on Employment, Manpower, and Poverty of the Committee on Labor and Public Welfare, Washington: U. S. Senate, 1968.

74. _____. "Evaluating Manpower Programs," *Monthly Labor Review*, February 1968.

75. _____. *MDTA: Foundations of Federal Manpower Policy.* Baltimore: The Johns Hopkins Press, 1968.

76. _____. "Manpower Programs in the Antipoverty Effort," *Examination of the War on Poverty*, Vol. II. Staff and consultants' reports prepared for the Subcommittee on Employment, Manpower and Poverty of the Committee on Labor and Public Welfare. Washington: U. S. Senate, August 1967.

77. _____. *Reorienting Vocational Education.* Ann Arbor: Institute of Labor and Industrial Relations, University of Michigan and Wayne State University, 1968.

78. Mann, E. T. and Elliott, C. C. "Assessment of the Utility of Project Head Start for the Culturally Deprived: An Evaluation of Social and Psychological Functioning," *Training School Bulletin*, February 1968.

79. Mao, James C. T. "Efficiency in Public Urban Renewal Expenditures through Benefit-Cost Analysis," *Journal of the American Institute of Planners*, March 1966.

80. Marshall Kaplan, Gans & Kahn. *Effectiveness Evaluation: Section 701 Local Urban Planning Assistance Program*. Washington: September 1967.

81. Mass, A. "Benefit-Cost Analysis: Its Relevance to Public Investment Decisions," *Quarterly Journal of Economics*, May 1966.

82. McKean, R. N. *Efficiency in Government through Systems Analysis*. New York: Wiley, 1968.

83. McKechnie, Graeme H. *Retraining and Geographic Mobility: An Evaluation*. Ph.D. dissertation. Madison: University of Wisconsin, 1966.

84. Michigan State University, School of Labor and Industrial Relations. *Retraining under the Manpower Development Training Act–A Study of Attributes of Trainees Associated with Successful Retraining*. Prepared for Department of Labor, Manpower Administration. East Lansing: January 1968.

85. Miller, S. M. "The Study of Man: Evaluating Action Programs," *Transaction*, March-April 1965.

86. Morrison, James W. "A Comprehensive Evaluation Model for Community Action Programs." Paper prepared for 1966 annual meeting, Society for the Study of Social Problems. Miami, Florida: August 26-29, 1966.

87. Mosely, Donald C. and Williams, D. C., Jr. *An Analysis and Evaluation of a Community Action Anti-Poverty Program in the Mississippi Delta*. State College, Mississippi: College of Business and Industry, Mississippi State University, July 1967.

88. Muir, Allen, et al. *Cost/Effectiveness Analysis of On-the-Job and Institutional Training Courses*. Washington: Planning Research Corp., June 1967.

89. Muth, Richard. *The Evaluation of Present and Potential Poverty Programs*. Arlington, Virginia: Institute for Defense Analyses, January 1966.

90. _____. *An Evaluation of the Reduction in Poverty among Various Demographic Groups, 1947 to 1963*. Arlington, Virginia: Institution for Defense Analyses, June 1966.

91. National Advisory Council on the Education of Disadvantaged Children. *Title I–ESEA: A Review and a Forward Look–1969*. Washington: Government Printing Office, 1969.

92. Nemore, A. L. "Transferability of Manpower Programs," *Examination of the War on Poverty*. Vol. II. Staff and consultants' reports prepared for the Subcommittee on Employment, Manpower and Poverty of the Committee on Labor and Public Welfare, U. S. Senate. Washington, D. C.: U. S. Senate, August 1967.

93. _____. and Mangum, Garth L. *Reorienting the Federal-State Employment Service* (Policy Papers in Human Resources and Industrial Relations,

No. 8). Ann Arbor: Institute of Labor and Industrial Relations, University of Michigan and Wayne State University, May 1968.

94. New York Center for Study of the Unemployed. *Study of the Meaning, Experience and Effect of the Neighborhood Youth Corps on Negro Youths Who Are Seeking Work,* Part V. Prepared for the Office of Economic Opportunity. New York: June 1968.

95. Nosow, Sigmund. *Retraining under the MDTA Act.* East Lansing: School of Labor and Industrial Relations, Michigan State University, January 1968.

96. Nourse, Hugh O. "The Economics of Urban Renewal," *Land Economics,* February 1966.

97. Office of Economic Opportunity. *Applying for a CAP Grant.* Washington: August 1968.

98. _____. CAP Research and Development Division. *Fiscal Year 1969 Plan.* Washington: October 1968.

99. _____. *Contracts Executed through December 31, 1967.* Internal administrative paper. Washington: 1968.

100. _____. CAP. *Management Information Reporting by Community Action Agencies, Grantee Reporting Manual.* Washington: July 1967.

101. _____. *Organizing Communities for Action under the 1967 Amendments to the Economic Opportunity Act.* Washington: February 1968.

102. _____. Office of Research, Plans, Programs, and Evaluation. *Research Project to Analyze the Effects of Community Action.* Washington: 1968.

103. _____. *Evaluation Manual, Legal Services Programs.* Washington: August 1967.

104. _____. *Standards for Evaluating the Effectiveness of Community Action Programs.* Washington: May 1969.

105. Organization for Social and Technical Innovation, Inc. *An Assessment of Six Labor Mobility Demonstration Projects.* Cambridge, Massachusetts: November 1967.

106. Ott, Jack M. "Classification System for Decision Situations: An Aid to Educational Planning and Evaluation," *Educational Technology,* February 1969.

107. PACE. *PACE Report, A Look at Evaluation.* Lexington: College of Education, University of Kentucky, 1967.

108. Page, D. A. "Retraining under the Manpower Development Act: A Cost-Benefit Analysis," *Public Policy,* Vol. 13, 1964.

109. Pennsylvania State University, Institute for Research in Human Resources. *A Cost Effectiveness Study of Vocational Education: A Com-*

parison of Vocational and Non-Vocational Education in Secondary Schools. University Park, Pennsylvania: March 1969.

110. Peters, G. H. *Cost-Benefit Analysis and Public Expenditure.* London: London Institute of Economic Affairs, 1966.

111. Polgar, Steven and Kaffe, F. S. "Evaluation and Record Keeping for U. S. Family Planning Services," *Public Health Reports,* August 1968.

112. Posner, James. *Evaluation of Successful Projects in Compensatory Education.* Washington: Department of Health, Education and Welfare, Office of Planning and Evaluation, April 10, 1968.

113. The President's Task Force on Manpower Conservation. *One-Third of a Nation.* Washington: Department of Labor, January 1, 1964.

114. Price Waterhouse and Co. *Management Actions Required for Improved Project Administration.* New York: September 1968.

115. Rapkin, Chester and Grigsby, William G. *Residential Renewal in the Urban Core.* Philadelphia: University of Pennsylvania Press, 1959.

116. Real Estate Research Corporation. *Study and Report of the Effectiveness of Urban Planning in Communities under 50,000 Population, HUD Region IV.* Prepared for Department of Housing and Urban Development. Washington: 1967.

117. Resource Management Corp. *Evaluation of the War on Poverty: Education Programs.* Prepared for General Accounting Office. Bethesda, Maryland: March 1969.

118. _____. *Evaluations of the War on Poverty–The Feasibility of Benefit-Cost Analysis for Manpower Programs.* Prepared for General Accounting Office. Bethesda, Maryland: March 1969.

119. Ribich, Thomas. *Education and Poverty.* Washington: The Brookings Institution, 1968.

120. Rivlin, Alice M. and Wholey, Joseph S. "Education of Disadvantaged Children," *Socio-Economic Planning Sciences,* Vol. 2, 1969.

121. Rockwell, Richard C. *A Study of the Law and the Poor in Cambridge, Massachusetts: Attitudes and Perceptions, and Use of the Legal System.* Cambridge: Harvard University, June 1968.

122. Ross, William B. "A Proposed Methodology for Comparing Federally Assisted Housing Programs," *American Economic Review,* May 1967.

123. Rossi, Peter H. "Practice, Method, and Theory in Evaluating Social Action Programs." Johns Hopkins. (Unpublished.) March 1968.

124. _____. and Dentler, Robert A. *The Politics of Urban Renewal: The Chicago Findings.* New York: Free Press, 1961.

125. Rothenberg, Jerome. *Economic Evaluation of Urban Renewal*. Washington: The Brookings Institution, 1967.

126. Schaaf, A. H. *Economic Aspects of Urban Renewal: Theory, Policy, and Area Analysis*. Research Report 14, Real Estate Research Program, Institute of Business and Economic Research. Berkeley: University of California, 1960.

127. Schmelzer, June L., ed. *Learning in Action, Selected Issues in Training and Demonstration Projects*. Washington: Department of Health, Education and Welfare, Office of Juvenile Delinquency and Youth Development, 1966.

128. Schusshiem, Morton. "Determining Priorities in Urban Renewal," *Papers and Proceedings of the Regional Science Association*. Philadelphia: 1960.

129. Shellhammer, T. "ESEA, Title I, Compensatory Education Projects; with Special Reference to Program Evaluation," *California Education*, January 1966.

130. E. F. Shelley and Co., Inc. *Private Industry and the Disadvantaged Worker*. Prepared for the Urban Coalition. New York: January 1969.

131. _____. *Summary of Regional and State Analysis of Research and Pilot Projects*. Prepared for the Office of Economic Opportunity. New York: April 8, 1968.

132. Sheps, Cecil, M.D., and Madison, Donald L., M.D. *Evaluation of Neighborhood Health Centers—A Plan for Implementation*. Prepared for the Office of Economic Opportunity. New York: Mount Sinai Medical School, July 1967.

133. Sherwood, Clarence C. *Issues in Measuring Results of Action Programs*. Chicago: National Conference on Social Welfare, June 1966.

134. Slayton, William L. "State and Local Incentives and Techniques for Urban Renewal," *Law and Contemporary Problems*, Autumn 1960.

135. Software Systems, Inc. *A Job Corps Case Study of Relative Cost-Benefits*. Washington: April 1969.

136. Somers, Gerald G. "Our Experience with Retraining and Relocation," in R. A. Gordon, ed., *Toward a Manpower Policy*. New York: John Wiley & Sons, 1967.

137. _____. *Retraining the Unemployed*. Madison: University of Wisconsin Press, 1968.

138. Stromsdorfer, Ernst W. "Determinants of Economic Success in Retraining the Unemployed: The West Virginia Experience," *Journal of Human Resources*. Vol. III, No. 2, Spring 1968.

139. _____. and Cain, Glen G. "An Economic Evaluation of the Government Retraining of the Unemployed in West Virginia, 1965." (Mimeo.)

140. Stumpf, Harry P. "Law and Poverty; a Political Perspective," *Wisconsin Law Review*, 1968.

141. _____. *Study of OEO Legal Services Programs, Bay Area, California*. Albuquerque: University of New Mexico, September 1968.

142. Suchman, Edward A. *Evaluative Research. Principles and Practice in Public Service and Social Action Programs*. New York: Russell Sage Foundation, 1967.

143. Swanson, J. Chester and Arnold, Walter M. "A New Look at Vocational-Technical Education," *State Government*, Summer 1968.

144. Task Force on Occupational Training in Industry. Report: *A Government Commitment to Occupational Training in Industry*. Washington: Government Printing Office, August 1968.

145. Trooboff, Benjamin M. *Employment Experience after MDTA Training*. Atlanta: School of Business Administration, Georgia State College, July 1968.

146. U. S. Congress, Joint Economic Committee. *The Analysis and Evaluation of Public Expenditures: The PPB System*. Washington: Government Printing Office, 1969.

147. _____. *Economic Analysis and the Efficiency of Government*. Washington: Government Printing Office, 1970.

148. U. S. Department of Health, Education and Welfare, Office of Education, *An Analysis of Vocational Education in Our Secondary Schools*. Washington: July 1967.

149. _____. *The Bridge between Man and His Work*. General Report of the Advisory Council on Vocational Education. Washington: 1968.

150. _____. *Education and Training–A Chance to Advance*. Washington: Government Printing Office, April 1969.

151. _____. *Education for a Changing World of Work*. Report of the Panel of Consultants on Vocational Education. Washington: Government Printing Office, 1964.

152. _____. *1969 Survey on Compensatory Education*. Washington: 1969.

153. _____. *Child Development: Summary of the Child Development Task Force Report*. Washington: April 1968.

154. _____. *Vocational Education*. General Report of the Advisory Council on Vocational Education. Washington: 1968.

155. U. S. Department of Labor, Bureau of Labor Statistics. *Counselor's Guide to Manpower Information: An Annotated Bibliography of Government Publications.* Washington: U. S. Government Printing Office, September 1968.

156. _____. Manpower Administration, Division of Planning. *The Employment Effects of Manpower Development Programs: A Model.* Washington: November 17, 1967.

157. _____. *The Influence of MDTA Training on Earnings.* Washington: Government Printing Office, 1968.

158. _____. Manpower Administration. *Manpower Development and Training in Correctional Programs.* Washington: 1968.

159. _____. *Manpower Report of the President, 1968.* Washington: Government Printing Office, 1968.

160. _____. *Manpower Report of the President, 1969.* Washington: Government Printing Office, 1969.

161. _____. Manpower Administration. *Manpower Research Projects through June 30, 1968.* Washington: October 1968.

162. _____. Manpower Administration, Bureau of Work-Training Programs. *The Neighborhood Youth Corps—Three Years of Success.* Washington: 1968.

163. _____. *Statistics on Manpower, A Supplement to the Manpower Report of the President.* Washington: Government Printing Office, 1969.

164. U. S. General Accounting Office. *Review of Economic Opportunity Programs.* Report to Congress. Washington: Government Printing Office, March 1969.

165. U. S. House of Representatives, Committee on Education and Labor. *Hearings on the Extension of Elementary and Secondary Programs,* Part IV. Washington: Government Printing Office, 1969.

166. _____. Special Subcommittee on Education. *Study of the United States Office of Education.* Washington: Government Printing Office, 1967.

167. U. S. Senate, Committee on Government Operations, Subcommittee on Intergovernmental Relations. *Criteria for Evaluation in Planning State and Local Problems: A Study.* Washington: Government Printing Office, 1967.

168. _____. Committee on Labor and Public Welfare. *Examination of the War on Poverty: Hearings before the Subcommittee on Employment, Manpower, and Poverty of the Committee on Labor and Public Welfare,* Government Printing Office, 1967.

169. University of Pittsburgh, "Follow Through Evaluation Project—Interim Report." (Unpublished.) March 1968.

170. Vincent, Howard. *Exemplary Vocational Program for the Disadvantaged*. An experimental program with federal funds. Washington: Office of Education, Office of Program Planning and Evaluation, March 1969.

171. Walther, Regis H. and Magnusson, Margaret L. *A Retrospective Study of the Effectiveness of Out-of-School Neighborhood Youth Corps Programs in Four Urban Sites*. Prepared for Department of Labor, Office of Manpower Policy, Evaluation and Research. Washington: Social Research Group, The George Washington University, November 1967.

172. Weisbrod, Burton A. *Benefits of Manpower Programs: Theoretical and Methodological Issues*. Madison: University of Wisconsin, May 14, 1969.

173. Weiss, Carol. *Utilization of Evaluation; Toward Comparative Study*. Paper presented at the American Sociological Association meeting. Miami Beach: American Sociological Association, September 1, 1966.

174. Westinghouse Learning Corporation-Ohio University. *The Impact of Head Start: Evaluation of the Effects of Head Start on Children's Cognitive and Affective Development*. July 12, 1969.

175. Wheeler, Ben. "Relative Cost-Benefits Analysis of Job Corps Training Programs." (Unpublished.) September 1968.

176. Wildavsky, Aaron. *The Politics of the Budgeting Process*. Boston: Little, Brown and Co., 1964.

177. Williams, Walter. "Developing an Agency Evaluation Strategy for Social Action Programs." *The Journal of Human Resources*, Vol. IV, No. 4, Fall 1969.

178. _____. "Science and Social Policy-Making." Unpublished manuscript, 1970.

179. Williams, Walter and Evans, John W. "The Politics of Evaluation: The Case of Head Start," *Annals of the American Academy of Political and Social Science*, September 1969.

180. Wilson, Alan B. "Residential Segregation of Social Classes and Aspirations of High School Boys," *American Sociological Review*, December 1959.

181. Wilson, James Q. "Urban Renewal Does Not Always Renew," *Harvard Today*, January 1965.

182. _____, ed. *Urban Renewal: The Record and the Controversy*. Cambridge: Massachusetts Institute of Technology Press, 1966.

183. Wingo, Lowdon, Jr. "Urban Renewal: Objectives, Analyses, and Information Systems," in Werner Z. Hirsch, ed., *Regional Accounts for Policy Decisions*. Baltimore: John Hopkins Press, 1966.

184. Winnick, Louis. "Economic Questions in Urban Redevelopment," *American Economic Review*, May 1961.

185. _____. "Facts and Fictions in Urban Renewal," in *Ends and Means of Urban Renewal*, papers from the Philadelphia Housing Association's Fiftieth Anniversary Forum. Philadelphia: Philadelphia Housing Association, 1961.

186. Wolfers, D. "An Evaluation Criterion for a National Family Planning Program," *American Journal of Public Health*, August 1968.

187. Yankelovich (Daniel), Inc. *CAP Programs and Their Evaluation: A Management Report*. Prepared for the Office of Economic Opportunity. New York: September 1967.

Urban Institute Reports

3-107-1   *A Directory of University Urban Research Centers* (January
1970, 141 pp, LC 72-112409, $3.50), Reed Martin, Editor

5-301-4   *Urban Processes: As Viewed by the Social Sciences* (March
1970, 79 pp, LC 73-120085, $1.95), Kenneth J. Arrow, James
G. March, James S. Coleman, Anthony Downs and William Gorham

8-112-5   *Operating Costs in Public Housing: A Financial Crisis* (September 1969, 63 pp. LC 74-129111, $1.50), Frank deLeeuw and
Eleanor Littman Tarutis

9-121-21   *Federal Evaluation Policy: Analyzing the Effects of Public Pro-
grams* (June 1970, 134 pp, LC 78-139578, $2.95), Joseph S.
Wholey, John W. Scanlon, Hugh G. Duffy, James S. Fukumoto,
Leona M. Vogt

10-112-6   *Thinking about Housing: A Policy Research Agenda* (May 1970,
47 pp, LC 75-134845, $1.25), Morton L. Isler

31-113-26 *The Monetary Rewards of Migration within the U.S.* (March
1970, 62 pp, LC 74-140316, $1.95), Richard F. Wertheimer II

32-112-15 *Property Taxation, Housing and Urban Growth: With Attention
to Tax Reform and Assessment Modernization* (June 1970, 72
pp, LC 78-140317, $2.50), Walter Rybeck, Moderator

33-116-12 *University Training in PPB for State and Local Officials* (August
1970, 92 pp, LC 70-141757, $3.50), Selma J. Mushkin, Moder-
ator

37-108-67 *Measuring the Effectiveness of Local Government Services:
Solid Waste Collection* (October 1970, 36 pp, $2.00), Louis H.
Blair, Harry P. Hatry, Pasqual A. DonVito

38-350-27 *The Unemployment-Inflation Dilemma: A Manpower Solution*
(November 1970, 112 pp, LC 77-149809, $2.95), Charles C.
Holt, C. Duncan MacRae, Stuart O. Schweitzer, Ralph E. Smith

55-108-70 *The Indianapolis Police Fleet Plan: An Example of Program
Evaluation for Local Government* (October 1970, 59 pp,
$2.00), Donald M. Fisk

56-108-69 *Measuring the Effectiveness of Local Government Services:
Recreation* (January 1971, 47 pp, LC 76-155067, $1.75), Harry
P. Hatry, Diana R. Dunn

68-108-73 *The Struggle to Bring Technology to Cities* (May 1971, 80 pp,
LC 71-156316, $1.95)

72-108-65 *Introduction to Sample Surveys for Government Managers*
(April 1971, 48 pp, LC 79-160422, $1.50), Carol H. Weiss,
Harry P. Hatry

Urban Institute Papers

102-1   *Citizen Participation: A Review and Commentary on Federal Policies and Practices* (September 1969, 122 pp, $3.00), Melvin B. Mogulof

102-6   *Quality of the Urban Environment: The Federal Role* (May 1970, 83 pp, $3.00), Elizabeth H. Haskell

102-13   *Urban Waste Management: The Federal Role* (May 1970, 95 pp, $3.00), Elizabeth H. Haskell

112-11   *Income and the Cost of Rental Housing* (January 1970, 44 pp, $2.00), Frank deLeeuw and Nkanta F. Ekanem

112-14   *The Demand for Housing: A Review of Cross-Section Evidence* (March 1970, 42 pp, $2.00), Frank deLeeuw and Nkanta F. Ekanem

112-19   *Time Lags in the Rental Housing Market* (June 1970, 57 pp, $2.50), Frank deLeeuw and Nkanta F. Ekanem

112-25   *The Design of a Housing Allowance* (October 1970, 42 pp, $2.00), Frank deLeeuw, Sam H. Leaman, Helen Blank

113-23   *Nonwhite Grains–Present Policy Trends* (August 1969, 24 pp, $1.00), Harvey A. Garn

113-30   *New Cities, New Communities and Growth Centers* (March 1970, 17 pp, $1.00), Harvey A. Garn

113-31   *Labor Market Analysis and Public Policy* (January 1970, 23 pp, $1.00), Harvey A. Garn

113-32   *Occupational Patterns in Urban Employment Change* (January 1970, 34 pp, $2.00), Charlotte Fremon

119-1   *Design for a School Rating or Classification System* (March 1970, 34 pp, $2.00), Bayla F. White

136-1   *The Quality of Life in Metropolitan Washington, D.C.: Some Statistical Benchmarks* (March 1970, 82 pp, $3.00), Martin V. Jones and Michael J. Flax

138-5   *Citizen Participation: The Local Perspective* (March 1970, 188 pp, $3.00), Melvin B. Mogulof

350-11   *Foregone Earnings during Manpower Training* (January 1970, 20 pp, $1.00), Ralph E. Smith

450-6   *The Urban Transportation Problem: A Brief Analysis of Our Objectives and the Prospects for Current Proposals* (March 1970, 18 pp, $1.00), Martin Wohl

705-50   *Subsidy Proposal to Induce State and Local Retirement Funds to Invest in State and Local Securities* (August 1969, 13 pp, $1.00), Selma J. Mushkin and Harvey Galper